Advance Praise for *By Heart*

"A boy with no one to listen becomes a man in prison for life. He reads for the first time, and discovers his mind can be free.

A women poet enters prison to teach, becomes his first listener, and so begin twenty-five years of friendship between two gifted writers and poets.

The result is *By Heart*, a mutually-written book that will anger you, give you hope and break your heart. In other words, their book will open your heart."   —Gloria Steinem, American feminist, journalist, and social activist

"A portrait of prison and of the pursuit of art. An amazing combo, a compelling read . . . years later, acting in *Godot* on Broadway, I see how much the San Quentin production has meant to my view of the play."
                              —Bill Irwin, TONY winning actor, appeared in the Broadway
                              revival of *Waiting for Godot*

"This is a book about poetry, about struggle, about freedom and incarceration, and most of all about heart. It is a wonderful read."
                              —devorah major, San Francisco Poet Laureate 2002–2005

"*By Heart* leads us on a poignant journey into that space in ourselves where we finally find our own voice. Bravo Judith and Spoon for a beautiful work of art."
                              —Piri Thomas, writer, poet, author of *Down These Mean Streets*

"The collaboration between Judith Tannenbaum and Spoon Jackson continues the path to freedom through art. *By Heart* is so beautifully described, both objectively and emotionally."
                              —Barney Rosset, Publisher/Editor of Grove Press 1951–1985

"*By Heart* works on so many levels. We get to know both Judith and Spoon through that terrific 'eye' and 'I' revelation that memoir offers at its best."   —Rilla Askew, author of *Fire in Beulah* and other books

"A remarkable memoir of two powerful personalities brought together through poetry and prison. Through Judith's genuineness a poet awoke and found a way to live a fuller life in spite of confinement, and through Spoon's honesty and talent many people will be compelled to contribute to society, even if society has abandoned them."

—Joseph Lea, Library Media Specialist, York Correctional
Institution, Niantic, CT

"This double memoir is imperative for artists who understand the need to reveal and share our common humanity. Spoon Jackson's and Judith Tannenbaum's journeys through childhood, love, loss, and back to poetry move and astound me."

—Rhodessa Jones, Founder/Artistic Director of The Medea Project:
Theater for Incarcerated Women

"In their remarkable memoir, Spoon Jackson and Judith Tannenbaum show us how words change lives, how poetry invites you to free your mind, even in a maximum security prison.

—Ken Lamberton, author of *Wilderness and Razor Wire:*
A Naturalist's Observations from Prison and other books

BY HEART

BY HEART

Poetry, Prison, and Two Lives

Judith Tannenbaum
and
Spoon Jackson

New Village Press • Oakland, CA

Published by
New Village Press
P.O. Box 3049
Oakland, CA 94609

Orders: (510) 420-1361
press@newvillage.net
www.newvillagepress.net

New Village Press is a public-benefit, not-for-profit publishing venture
of Architects/Designers/Planners for Social Responsibility. www.adpsr.org

Printed in Canada by Friesens Corporation.

In support of the Greenpress Initiative, New Village Press is committed to
the preservation of endangered forests globally and advancing best practices
within the book and paper industries. The printing papers used in this book
are acid-free and have been certified with both the Forest Stewardship
Council (FSC) and the Sustainable Forestry Initiative (SFI).

ISBN-13 978-0-9815593-5-3
Publication Date: April 2010

Library of Congress Cataloging-in-Publication Data

Tannenbaum, Judith.
    By heart : poetry, prison, and two lives / Judith Tannenbaum and Spoon Jackson.
        p. cm.
    ISBN 978-0-9815593-5-3 (pbk. : alk. paper)
        1. Tannenbaum, Judith. 2. Poets, American—20th century—Biography.
3. Jackson, Spoon. 4. Prisoners—United States—Biography. I. Jackson, Spoon. II. Title.
    PS3620.A6865Z46 2010
    811'.54—dc22
    [B]   2010003858

Cover design by Adrienne Eliza Aquino.
Front cover photos from family album except the adult Spoon Jackson photo
    by Beppe Arvidsson.
Interior design and composition by Leigh McLellan Design.

Also by Judith Tannenbaum

Disguised as a Poem: My Years Teaching Poetry at San Quentin
Jump Write In! Creative Writing Exercises for Diverse Communities,
        Grades 6-12, with Valerie Chow Bush
Manual For Artists Working in Prison
Teeth, Wiggly as Earthquakes: Writing Poetry in the Primary Grades
Solid Ground, as editor

as contributor

An Invisible Rope: Portraits of Czeslaw Milosz, edited by
        Cynthia Haven
Fire & Ink: An Anthology of Social Action Writing, edited
        by Frances Payne Adler, Debra Busman, Diana Garcia
How to Make a Life as a Poet, edited by Gary Mex Glazner
Teaching the Arts behind Bars, edited by Rachel Marie-Crane Williams

poetry collections

In The Crook of Grief's Arm
No Longer Hers
Songs In The Night
Ten To Darkness
The Dark Thoughts
The World Saying Yes

Also by Spoon Jackson

as contributor

I Hear America Reading, edited by Jim Burke

poetry collections

Longer Ago
No Distance Between Two Points

Judith dedicates *By Heart* to a world
in which all children are our children.

And from Spoon for all the people—
young, old, artists, and prisoners: You can!

"You are human beings nonetheless.
As far as one can see.
Of the same species as myself."
POZZO, IN SAMUEL BECKETT'S *WAITING FOR GODOT*

Contents

Preface

Judith

IN THE 1980S, when Spoon was my student at San Quentin and discovering himself as a poet, he told me that he imagined the two of us giving a reading in Berkeley, working with children on their poems, or creating a poetry performance together. He told me that one day, we would. This prediction made me happy. However when I received a letter from Spoon in 2006 proposing that we write a two-person memoir, I set myself to say no.

For one thing, I'd already written a memoir about my years teaching at San Quentin, and there was no point in retelling the same story I'd told in *Disguised as a Poem*. For another, with Spoon still locked up, the tools we'd have for working together would make the process a big challenge. The letters between us would be read by staff and might take weeks to get through the mailroom. The timed collect telephone calls Spoon could place to me would be broken into by a recorded, robotic, message full of mechanical beeps and pronouncements. Besides, the last time Spoon had asked me to edit a long prose project he'd begun, we ended up furious with each other. So, as I say, I read Spoon's letter thinking no.

Still, I found myself nodding at his description of the dramatically different life paths that had brought each of us to poetry. For we share no demographic—not race, class, birth year, education, religion, or family history. Yet, as Spoon pointed out, our paths crossed and that crossing has led to a nearly twenty-five year conversation about poems, education, beauty, possibility, and what it means to be human.

Spoon ended his letter: "You believed in me even when you didn't know me." I looked up when I read those words. The gift of Spoon's statement sparked a dozen thoughts about what I feel is essential to good teaching, and I realized how much I wanted to write about these subjects—teaching, coming to poetry, believing in others. So instead of that no, I sat down at my desk and wrote yes to Spoon Jackson.

We worked like this: Spoon sent me the chapters he had written long-hand in his two-person cell. I typed up what he'd written, along with suggestions. He re-worked these chapters, mailed them back to me, and I added his changes to the typed script. This went on for a few rounds.

I sent my typed chapters to Spoon, too, as I wrote them. I wanted detailed response such as I was giving to him, but for a while he said only that what I'd written was fine, real, cool, and that he couldn't tell me how to write my own story. I complained and Spoon finally reminded me that he'd never before written an entire prose book; I had.

Memoir is a tricky genre, which Spoon and I have discussed as we've written this one. The form is non-fiction, so we're telling the truth. Spoon has argued more for truth's spirit and I've been more of a stickler, but we've agreed that memoir isn't journalism. For one thing, we have no doc-umented records. Neither of us taped conversations or transcribed them word-for-word in our journals and so every event we report is mediated through memory. We gave ourselves permission—not to make things up, not to write a novel and say that what we invented is what happened—but to recreate dialog and scene from what we remember.

Memory isn't a recording device, but works as poetry does, through image. The nature of image is to conflate, to thin at the edges, to resemble, merge, represent. Most adults have had the experience of speaking to a parent or sibling of a strong childhood memory, only to find out that the person with whom you shared the experience remembers the event as occurring at your grandmother's house and not at your aunt's as you recall. Your sister remembers you wearing a red shirt, your brother says it was plaid, your father insists harsh words were spoken, your mother remembers only laughter, and your cousin is sure the whole thing never happened. So Spoon and I, too, haven't always remembered what we shared in exactly the same way.

We two would never have met if not for Arts-in-Corrections, a pro-gram that places a professional artist as artist facilitator—a civil service position—in every California state prison. For the first two decades of the program's existence, the artist facilitator's job was to develop a cadre of paid practicing artists to offer fine arts instruction to prisoners. The program was slashed a number of years ago and it seemes Arts-in-Corrections and almost all programming will be eliminated from California prisons in 2010. As I write these words, though, Arts-in-Corrections still exists, and good artist facilitators continue to provide arts opportunities to men and women inside. Jim Carlson is more than good. Jim was a great artist facilitator at San Quentin where he worked when Spoon and I met and he's a great artist facilitator now at California State Prison-Sacramento—New Folsom—where Spoon is currently housed.

Back at San Quentin Spoon used to tell me, only partially in jest, that in introducing him to poetry I had saved his life. Therefore, he loved to remind me, I was forever responsible for the life I had saved. I don't feel responsible *for* Spoon, but I do feel responsible *to* him and to all my San Quentin students. We shared a lot in our four years together and in the twenty years since then. I have learned so much from these men, almost all of them still inside after three decades.

Spoon and I both feel responsible to young people coming up, as well as to men and women in prison. Spoon wants youth to know it's not cool to be caged; it is lonely, unnatural, painful, and a trap for the poor and people of color, a trap one may never be able to shake or get out of.

Spoon encourages everyone in prison to find the gift that frees his or her spirit and heart. He writes: "We must each do our part, despite the fact that our lives on the streets are only memories and dreams that may perish with us. Brothers and sisters—my people behind walls, no matter where you are around the world—walls cannot harness or stop our hearts, souls, and minds. Let your words, songs, and music flow. Keep it real and pass the realness on to others."

Acknowledgments

J UDITH AND SPOON begin by thanking each other. Spoon says that writing this book has been a journey, sometimes sad, happy, loving, and mad, but it has been all the time real. He thanks his big sis, Judith, for her endless labor to bring *By Heart* to light and for creating "the loop": a constant flow of printed emails, letters, and notes about sightings of his work that kept him inspired when he felt low. And Judith thanks Spoon for wanting to work on a project together, proposing that they write this book, holding hope, putting up with her stressed nature and non-stop letters, talking things out when they got frustrated with each other, and being the most reliable writing partner possible—always on task and on time.

Heartfelt thanks to Gloria Steinem for her encouragement and support and to Alexa Mergen for doing so much, over and over, to help us get the word out. Deepest gratitude to our readers: Rilla Askew, Elmo Chattman, Arlene Goldbard, Nick Jaffe, Sara Press, and Gail Todd. Tremendous thanks to Beppe Arvidsson, Albin Biblom, and Katharine Gin for generously allowing us to use their photographs; Barney Rosset, Astrid Rosset, and Steven Brower for the photo of Samuel Beckett; Abe Jackson for help gathering Spoon's family photos; Leigh McLellan for her beautiful book design and Adrienne Eliza Aquino for her great cover design; Michel Wenzer for creating films for our project; Kjell Nordeson for recording help for these films; and Jim Carlson for so much. Judith gives big thanks to the staffs, administrators, review panels, and other artist residents at Hedgebrook, Ragdale, the Virginia Center for the Creative Arts, and the Writers Colony at Dairy Hollow.

Judith treasures all her prison arts colleagues and thanks each and every one for the way that they and their work enrich her life. She also gives thanks to WritersCorps, the excellent program she's worked with for fifteen years. Judith is so grateful to have a job that asks her to share what she learned during her years as a community artist and that also gives her time to write. A warm shout out to all WritersCorps teachers over the years and an especially long, loud, and deep thank you to program manager, Janet Heller.

More thanks from Judith to her closest friends—Elmo Chattman, the Harber-Schrogins (Maxim, Karen, Jonah, and Julia), Barbara Naiditch, Gail Todd—and family: Andrew Harkness; Debbie, Jim, Emma, and Gus Ingebretsen; Edith Tannenbaum; the memory of Bob Tannenbaum; and always at the top of Judith's love-and-thanks list, her daughter, Sara Press.

Spoon gives gratitude to Mother Earth, his mom, his brother Abe, and his Peace G. family and friends in Sweden who have never stopped loving and inspiring him: Annika, Korina, Sanna, Jovanna, Simon, Daneila, Louise, Karin, Krister, Eva, Anna, Lisen, Jann, Michel, Harald, Stefan, Lena, Ingunn, Albin, Mimi, Sverker, and his second mom, Barbro. Spoon gives warm thanks to Samuel Beckett, Barney Rosset, Bill Irwin, Liz Irwin, and Jan Jonson.

Thank you to the wonderful New Village Press. Lynne Elizabeth and the whole New Village team have been fantastic to work with and we're so grateful for everyone's sincere interest in our story.

We thank the people who have shared our lives with us. We've changed a few names in By Heart, but not many.

Spoon speaks for both himself and Judith as he writes to his fellow prisoners and to young people around the world: "I hope you will continue to make a life out of nothingness. We are still alive and can create that whatever-it-is that frees our hearts and spirits."

Chapter Five: Stanislav Baranczak's "If you have to scream ..." is in Under My Own Roof, Mr. Cogito Press, 1980. Czeslaw Milosz's "Dedication" is in The Collected Poems, Ecco Press, 1988. Pablo Neruda's "To the Foot from Its Child" is in The Poetry of Pablo Neruda, Farrar, Strauss, and Giroux, 2005.

Chapter Seven: Gary Snyder's "Hay for the Horses" is in Riprap, Origin Press, 1959. Tu Fu's "Clear Evening After Rain" is in One Hundred Poems from the Chinese, Kenneth Rexroth editor, New Directions, 1971. Ogden Nash's The Adventures of Isabel was published as its own book by Little

Brown & Co., 1994. Victor Valle's "Comida" is in *Highlights for Children*, 2000. Lilian Moore's "Winter Dark" is in *Winter Poems,* Scholastic Publishers, 1999. The quote from James was recorded by Scoop Nisker and played on Kris Welch's Morning Show (radio station KPFA in Berkeley, California) on December 3, 1987.

Chapter Nine: James Wright "A Blessing" is in his *Collected Poems*, Wesleyan University Press, 1951. Emily Dickinson (341), *The Complete Poems of Emily Dickinson*, 1890. Robert Hass, "Spring Drawing II", *Human Wishes*, Ecco Press, 1989. Poems by Myrna Scott (used by permission of author) are from *Driftwood Shores*, 1981.

Chapter Eleven: Excerpts from *Waiting for Godot* by Samuel Beckett, copyright © 1954 by Grove Press, Inc.; copyright © renewed 1984 by Samuel Beckett. Used by permission of Grove/Atlantic, Inc. and Faber and Faber Ltd. The quote from film-maker, Robert Bresson, is from *Notes On Cinematography*, translated by Jonathan Griffin, 1977.

Chapter Sixteen: Lines from Walt Whitman ("Leaves of Grass") and Matthew Arnold ("Dover Beach") are in the public domain.

We have rewritten some material in *By Heart* from previous work:

Judith:
"Artistic Imperialism," *Poetry Flash*, 1987.
"Human Beings Together," *Turning Wheel*, 2003.
"In My Two Hands," coastnews.com, 1996.
 "Poetry, Teaching, and Love," *Memo: Arts*, 1989.
"Power or Prison," inmotionmagazine.com, 2007.

Spoon:
Life/Lines poetry.org, Academy of American Poets.
"On Prison Reform," *San Francisco Chronicle*, 2006.
"Right Now I Choose Sadness," *I Hear America Reading*, edited by Jim Burke, Heinemann Publishing, 1999.
"Speaking in Poems," *Teaching Artist Journal: Volume 5 Issue 1*, 2007.

1

This Near-Stranger's Words

"**N**INETY DEGREES hotter, I'd be warm," Spoon Jackson tells me. Spoon sits near the bottom of a circular metal staircase in front of San Quentin's education building. I stand, nervous as usual. Nervous not because this is prison, but because I'm always nervous. Nervous system nervous, nervous inside my skin. Skin now wet with the day's unusual heat. Spoon and I wait for the officer to arrive, to unlock the door with a key from his belt, and to let us inside.

Us: a tall, black man in his late twenties; a short, white woman ten years older.

"I'm from the Mohave, the heart of the high desert," Spoon says. A fact and, I assume, the cause of Spoon's love of swelter.

That anyone could want this hot day even hotter is shocking enough. More shocking still are all these words from Spoon's lips. Spoon? The man who has spoken so little in our poetry class this past year? I'm too hot to express my surprise with any grand flourish but I'm definitely surprised. I don't know what Spoon notes on my face. His eyes are hidden by sunglasses, as usual, and I can't see what he feels. We're in pause-mode as we wait for the guard: small talk instead of conversation, silence (Spoon), smiles (me).

We wait and men move all around us. Mostly men dressed in blue denim, the blue that Spoon wears. A fair number of men in green. For example, the guard walking toward us. A few women, too, wear the green uniform. Some people are dressed, as I am, in street clothes. This Wednesday I wear a long flowered skirt, a turquoise shirt, Birkenstock sandals. *Hippie* both prisoners and guards tease me.

Movement, Afternoon Movement. That's how this time of day is referred to at San Quentin. Most prisoners' jobs are now over and the men in blue are on their way back to their cells or to workshops and classes that run until count clears, an imprecise moment that usually occurs between four thirty and five.

I've been teaching poetry at the prison for just over one year, and what I know of San Quentin is Monday nights: the sight of boats on the bay as I walk from the parking lot toward the castle-like structure ahead; the sound of guards joking as they go through the papers I carry; the creak of metal gates opening to let me inside, the clang as they shut; birdsong in the tree in front of the captain's porch at the edge of what's called the garden plaza; the slight dungeon-y smell of the education building and our basement classroom; prison place names: Yard Side, Bay Side, West Block, Four Post, Max Shack, the Upper Yard; walking through the last gate after class is over and hearing the sound of the bay lap the rocky shore, as though along the promenade in Nice or some other Riviera town. I know the men in my class—Angel and his jeremiads, Coties' concern for his children, Elmo's intelligence and strength, Spoon nearly silent. I know what they tell me, their writing, the poems and conversations we share. I know something and know this something isn't much.

Now, this very day, begins the expansion of my poetry program from Monday nights to twenty hours each week. One element of this expansion is the addition of weekly conversations with one, then another, of my students. I've chosen to meet first with Spoon because he is the man I'm most curious about—he's in class every Monday though he says nearly nothing and shows us few poems. What is he getting from our workshop, I wonder. Why does Spoon come to class every week?

The officer finally arrives. He checks Spoon's name on the movement sheet, takes his ID card, and waves us downstairs. I expected that I would have to do all the talking, but as we walk past the window that frames Mount Tamalpais, Spoon tells me how, as a boy, he'd stand on Crooks Street and look out at the mountains. "I thought those hills held the whole world," Spoon says as we descend the staircase. "How naïve was I."

I carry a bundle of poems in case Spoon has brought none of his own. But as we walk along the basement hallway, I note the cardboard container Spoon carries. I'm prepared with poetry talk, but once we're inside the classroom, Spoon empties his makeshift briefcase and spreads file folders out on the table between us. I have readied a speech about the purpose of these individual consultations, but before I begin, Spoon reaches into a folder and hands me a thick stack of poems.

Spoon removes the sunglasses I've never seen him without and looks toward the heavily barred window through which some late afternoon late summer light falls. The room is so quiet with only the two of us in it, though I hear prisoner musicians play with their teacher, Malonga, at the end of the hall and boot steps as the guards patrol outside the classroom.

I swoon the internal swoon that I hope will allow me to settle. I try to shut it all out—the shaft of bright light in the basement's darkness, the drumbeats, the boots—in order to focus on Spoon's poems, to bring myself to this near-stranger's words, and to enter the world these words introduce. Greyhounds, rabbits, railroad tracks, a small boy alone on B Hill. Twenty or thirty poems. No poem yet masterly, no poem ready to be proclaimed, but clearly Spoon—behind his dark shades—was not simply sleeping during our Monday night class.

My mind races. A cliché, as I'd note to any student. A cliché and also accurate - my mind does race. I hear the buzz of its motor, feel its incessant forward motion. I affirm, remark, praise, ask questions, offer a few suggestions. Mentally I go through my poetry library at home to see which books Spoon might want to read. I assess what formal material about poetics might be most useful. I talk to Spoon about the power of the concrete, pointing to lines in his poems, to particular phrases: those greyhounds, rabbits, and railroad tracks. When I get home, I've already decided, I'll type up the words Spoon spoke in this hour together. I want Spoon to hear his actual voice on the page. *The city jail's across from the high school, and I couldn't see but I heard the sounds of the games, those football games I'd gone to my whole life in that town.* I want him to note the details of his own stories. *My nephew wrote me a letter, first time in the ten years I've been here. He wrote he remembers I taught him to drive, to whistle. He remembers us washing my car. He wrote, "Dear Uncle Stanley."*

I see Spoon: his slight mustache and beard, his wide nose, light reflected off his dark skin. I hear Spoon's speech, a slow slur of sound different from any I know. Not urban, not old time Southern. Some kind of country, I guess. Spoon's words run together and it takes me awhile to find how to listen.

Although I'm most conscious of what's right before me—the physical fact of Spoon Jackson, the words he speaks and the poems he's written— my attention is also caught by more subtle matters. Space, for example. My happiness and surprise, as well as my effort to understand every word Spoon speaks, tilt my body forward. Spoon's words reach out, too. A little, at least. His body, though, rests against the back of his wooden chair. The space between us—space I lean into, space Spoon reclines at the edge of— creates its own story. What am I saying to Spoon with my forward motion? What is he saying to me with his apparently casual slouch?

"Pay attention," I've exhorted most weeks in class. "A poet's task is to pay attention."

And my students have laughed. "Judith, when we came down the stairs tonight, did you notice that the garbage can is no longer by the computer lab, but right next to our classroom?" one or another has asked me. "Did you see that the light was dimmer than usual in front of the music room? Did you hear how quietly those cops whispered on their way down the hall?"

I shake my head no.

"And *you're* telling *us* to pay attention?"

So I know, although we're saying nothing about it, that Spoon is noting as I am the space between us and the way this space shifts as we talk. I know the speed at which I ask question after question speaks some story to Spoon. As does my smile, as does the folded sheet of paper I use as a fan. But what? What story?

Prison rules might want me to remove everything that is not neutral and reduce this encounter to only the dictionary meaning of the words Spoon and I speak. But poetry isn't only dictionary meaning and neither is life. Poetry and life are both filled with connotation. I don't know Spoon well enough yet to even imagine what connotations he might bring to this exchange we're now in the midst of. I trip over my feet—metaphorically, imagistically—trying to avoid any pitfalls concealed by all this unknown nuance. No wonder I'm always nervous: doing my best to skirt trouble I can sense as possibility but not see as fact, to plan beforehand, and to notice exit routes just in case.

Here's an example, arranging a classroom. Teaching is thought of as imparting knowledge or skills. As inspiration, maybe. Lesson plans, assign-

4

ments, evaluation, class management. All relevant, of course. But also relevant is how the room is set up. At first I pulled two heavy tables together in our Monday night classroom and we all sat around the rectangular surface. This seating created its own equality. Or it seemed so to me. Then we were given a room with wooden desk-chairs, which I placed in a circle. The men didn't like my arrangement, though, and moved their seats into informal rows leaving me to the teacher's desk in front of the room. I guess my students wanted me to claim more professorial authority than I did when left to my own what-do-you-think, Socratic-questioning, Power-to-the-People instincts.

In class, Spoon took seating arrangements into his own hands. Literally. He lifted wooden chairs and carried them to the doorway where he constructed a half-circle of chairs as a perimeter he sat down within. Spoon was in class, but on his own terms. Some teacher might mind, might insist Spoon join the group. I didn't. I didn't mind and I didn't insist. Another artist teaching at the prison told me that Spoon scared him. Spoon didn't scare me. After all I was shy and liked being on the periphery, too. Besides, who says equality requires uniformity? *From each according to his ability, to each according to his need.* I wasn't a Marxist, but this phrase of Marx's seemed to me central to good teaching practice.

I often laughed at myself, or Fate, or whatever force had me standing so often in front of a group. I hated groups. Not hated, but groups made me uncomfortable and leading them made me a bit woozy. For one task of being a teacher is to welcome each individual, while simultaneously tracking the group as a whole. Offering the floor to each student *and* keeping things moving is two things, and doing two things at once, as I say, made me dizzy.

Still, this dizzy dance is one a teacher must master. When a kindergarten girl in the class circle launches into a detailed account of her grandmother's visit, a teacher's obligation is to listen with excitement while at the same time to skillfully offer the floor to the next child with his hand in the air waving like mad. When Spoon Jackson sat in his half-circle of chairs, I affirmed his right to separate from the group while simultaneously including him: making eye contact, mentioning his name, asking if he could see the videotaped poetry reading I had just put on the VCR.

This September afternoon, Spoon and I meet for our first individual consultation; I am thirty-nine years old and my work life, for more than a decade, has been anchored in the belief that making art is a human birth-right. Creating, I believe, is not only the province of an artist in his garret, but also of children, hospital patients, soldiers, drug addicts, cowboys, and old folk. And the province of prisoners, too.

So I put myself in front of groups of children, old folk, and prison-ers. We read poems together, write poems, study poetics, and converse about the world—the smell of a pippin apple in October and the nature of time, the taste of a grandmother's pecan pie and what we mean when we write the word "love."

Although I do all I know to welcome the *us* my pedagogy honors, in my heart of hearts I believe writing is a solo journey. So I am most grate-ful to have been granted the residency I am now beginning. Its promise of twenty hours each week at the prison means that I can add individual consultations, such as this one with Spoon, into my weekly schedule. My curiosity now will have plenty of room. I'll have time to ask: Who is this person, my student? What are his loves, interests, and responses to the world? Which writers, poems, artwork, and theories might move him? The residency will give me time to listen and to read each student's work so I can at least catch a glimpse of his path. And then more time to find mate-rial—books, single poems, recorded poetry readings—he might respond to.

Right now Spoon Jackson is before me, and I turn from my thoughts to the man. Twenty-nine years old, Spoon started serving a life without pos-sibility of parole sentence when he was twenty. My daughter has recently turned sixteen. For the sharp slice of one moment, I imagine that Sara has fewer than four years more to live in the world, that at twenty she might end up in prison or disappear in some way. No! I throw a mental screen down fast on the thought. I will not imagine that. No!

How can I hold that No!—a human reaction that makes me want to turn away—and still say Yes to Spoon Jackson? How can I feel for Spoon's fate, and the harm he caused that shaped that fate, and yet not be washed away by emotion? A Goldilocks question about finding "just right" between the poles of too much and too little. And also another task of a teacher not often listed alongside lesson plans and the rest. Right now, in this basement classroom, does "just right" require more distance? I could turn Spoon Jackson into a story. I love stories and Spoon has just shared an epic about a young man's path from high school to state prison; from the heart of the high desert to San Quentin, the infamous Bastille by the Bay.

Or does "just right" require less distance? If so, I have to rouse myself from all this thinking and look at the human being on the other side of the table, the one whose eyes slide everywhere except toward my face. This twenty-nine-year-old man I've been talking with since 3:30. Real, no story. Dark skin, broad nose, a heart beating under his blue prisoner's shirt. Spoon Jackson. A near stranger now slightly less strange.

2

In Silence

INDIAN SUMMER at San Quentin and the sweet sun brings back the times I ran the dry river with the greyhound dogs and lay under the heavy black railroad bridge as the trains rumbled across, shaking the soft sands. In those times, I watched the shadows of the railcars dart by, and when night fell on a hot day, played kick-the-can in pure desert darkness. There were no streetlights on Crooks Street when I was a boy.

My skin feels warm and alive this San Quentin September, as though I am a lizard sunning on a big rock. Instead I wear prison blues—shirt, pants, coat—plus brown high-top boots and dark shades, the coat and the shades I put on whenever I am outside the cell. I sit in my spot on the winding metal stairs of the San Quentin education building and see Judith bouncing down the steps from the Arts-in-Corrections office. I notice her healthy pale skin, small feet, slightly curly brown hair, long flowered skirt, and tire-track sandals.

Yes, I notice that Judith is a woman and at the same time a human being, struggling with life, death, truth, and imagination just as I am. She has already shown me new doors to step into, even in my silence, so I am able to absorb and appreciate that Judith is a woman in an all male prison, but also the leader and teacher of the poetry class.

This warm September afternoon, Judith is not as much a stranger to me as I am to her, for she has had to put herself out there to be credible. I have watched and listened to her share her truth, views, life, wisdom, and poetry. I know her through the books she suggested, the poetry she read aloud, and the ways she related to the others in the poetry class.

I have been through many summers in prison by this particular September. I arrived in 1977 from a small, desert town and have walked in dark shades and silence most of the time since then. None of the other prisoners, guards, or free staff has had a clue to what I am about or what I am capable of doing. They have had my prison file, a few pages gathered hastily together by the court: a probation officer, a couple of detectives, and a psychologist who, after one or two ten-minute sessions, purported to access, reveal, depict, and predict my entire life in one brush stroke. In that file was nothing about how my mom made me Arkansas meatloaf instead of cake for my birthday, a date we celebrated on August 21st instead of August 22nd for the first ten years of my life. Nothing in the file about how I spent time under Blacks Bridge, or how I ran the dry river with semi-wild dogs.

The guards, other prisoners, and prison staff could not place me anywhere, not in any street or prison gang. They did not know that I had learned to despise violence and to love peace, that I looked forward to lockdowns and to all the silence, reading, and studying given by those long stretches of time confined to my cell. When the cell door closed, doors to other places opened up. Prison people did not know that inside me was a desert thirst for knowledge—to know and explore new things.

Pre-prison, my life had never been one of words. I could barely read, and I spoke as my father did to me, in one-word sentences, shrugs, or by nodding my head. But during the months I was on trial, I sat stunned by all the words the DA used. I had no idea what these words meant and I told myself then that I would not let unknown words trap me. I started studying the dictionary in the county jail and reading all I could. I began to awaken the sleeping student inside me and took my first steps on my journey.

Once at San Quentin, I checked out all the books I could get from the prison library and education department. In one notebook I wrote down definitions. I used my favorite words in sentences in another notebook. I became enraptured with words and reading. I said certain words aloud many times and pondered a word in the way I thought of the garden in front of the prison chapel, or a sparrow singing in the tree by the captain's porch. I took all the adult high school education classes offered in the daytime. At night, I took all the college classes, self-help, and personal expansion programs offered: A Course in Miracles, Transcendental Meditation, and Toastmasters. All of these programs stressed taking responsibility for one's actions, forgiveness, growth, love, and peace.

I learned a few new words each day and each one brought a geyser erupting inside my mind and soul. The more words I read and studied, the clearer life became. I became richer and deeper inside. I could see, taste, feel, and touch the growth taking shape inside me and understood things I had never understood before. It was like I walked down an endless hallway full of dark rooms and each room I passed, a light came on and I learned something new. I had to choose to grow, which meant to get to know myself and find my niche, bliss, and myth in life. I had to till the endless gardens in my mind, heart, and soul.

I went into the cell on Friday afternoon and read and studied until Monday morning. I feasted on knowledge and wisdom. I dived into philosophy, religion, psychology, sociology, ecology, and any "ology" I could get my mind into. I debunked and peeled off layers of false history and propaganda that clogged my vision, my dreams, and my heart and soul—those misguided histories I had been force-fed like a motherless lamb.

For over eight years I had stayed to myself at San Quentin, learning who I was and what I was about. I avoided crowds. Although my heart, mind, and soul burned with thoughts, vibes, and feelings, I let none surface and stepped over wounded, dying, or dead bodies as everyone else did. Smiles only appeared when I was alone in the cell, writing or reading a letter. My teacher had become silence, and, through the wisdom silence brought, I had grown to feel happy and free inside.

But my journey was about to change and my life about to have a voice. On a whim, I signed up for two poetry classes. I had never read any poetry before, nor did I think I would like it. I had mistakenly thought that poetry was beyond me and only for women, squares, nerds, weirdos, professors, and highbrows, people caught up in some unreal academic world. Being incarcerated, I looked on poetry as a weakness, as was the expression of any feeling. I thought nothing true could come of it.

I would come to see that it took more heart to be a poet in prison than to be a gangster. When writing from a real place, even the appearance of poetry as soft became a strength and wielded power.

Judith taught one of the poetry classes and she suggested I jot down my thoughts and feelings, however those thoughts and feelings wanted to come out. She pronounced no "shoulds" or "should nots." I did the exercises, but kept the writing to myself. I sat in the back of the class with empty chairs surrounding me. Judith allowed me to absorb what I needed in silence, which made it possible to listen in the ways I needed to listen and to slowly transform inside. It was like setting a plant in a saucer of water to soak in what it needs for that moment. I do not know how she knew to leave me in silence but still somehow include me in the class. It might be her innate skills as an artist teacher to gauge and engage within each student their own inner voice. She knew what books to turn each student on to, the exact book that would enlighten. I learned that the universal truths able to touch souls and hearts are personal. With each class, I felt something freeing up inside me. Some emotion, some heart. Some wild unbreakable stallions that had been trapped in stalls were freed to roam the earth once again.

Having the doors of poetry opened to me by a woman was, I think, very important. As men in prison, we were caught up in a macho, masks-always-on, non-feeling world. In this setting, deep in one of the basement classrooms at San Quentin, having a woman artist teach me poetry was, at times, surreal. It allowed a full integration and expression of self through art.

My prison journey and my studies had taught me to observe the changes, the vibes, the sounds, and pitches that buzzed around me. I focused in on, or felt, everyone's gestures, voices, or moves. Silence gave me amazing focus and depth. I had heard Judith speak from the heart, nearly in tears, as some of the fellows in the group drilled her about her motives and reasons for coming inside San Quentin to teach. For me, either I trust somebody or I don't. I trusted Judith instantly and trusted what she had to offer and impart. I had no need to test, insult, or belittle her. What people are usually speaks like the sky.

Judith's words, and my fellow students' words, revealed a map to their minds, hearts, and souls. They were not nearly as much strangers to me as I was to them in my shades, chairs, and silence. This silence made many folks, including some prisoners and staff, wonder why I kept coming back after each Monday night class. The conversations, the lessons, as well as the observations I made, stretched my mind and deepened my heart. I felt more in tune with my own inner thoughts and world. When I went back to the cell after class, I read and wrote sometimes all night.

At first in my prison journey, I had just wanted to know what a word meant and how words were constructed into sentences so that high society and political folks like lawyers, doctors, and professors would not be able to say just anything and leave me not understanding. Now, in Judith's class, I began to embrace words in a new way and to allow words to embrace me. Words swarmed inside me like honeybees and took me places—imaginary and true—from the past, present, and future.

Almost everything I encountered in the poetry class was new, raw, inspiring, and fodder for my mind and heart to chew on. My journey had led me here, my whole life had become words—reading words, listening to words. Words slowly opened me up as I began to string them together, like swallows building their nests in spring. I had not learned yet how to stand out of the way and allow the muses to bring their gifts, but the gates of poetry had opened. There were so many images and visions inside me waiting for a way to come out, images and visions that must have lived within me—unrecognized—for decades.

For as a youngster, like a lot of young people in the free world, I lived on the edge of society, with no forum, form, or way to express what was on the inside. I had felt out of place in school, unheard and unseen. Though when I was about two-and-a-half tumbleweeds high, I looked out of my parents' bedroom window and watched some of my brothers and their friends prance across the field, stopping every so often, battling to establish leadership, playing follow-the-leader up into the sky over the railroad tracks. I knew the bridge they walked on led somewhere, maybe not over any rainbow, but to a place called school where all the kids older than I went. They seemed happy to go and they stayed all day long. I thought the fun must be endless.

I was five years old when I finally made it across the field and over the bridge. Kindergarten was fun. I liked the finger painting, the naps, the snacks, and playing at recess. I even loved my kindergarten teacher, Ms. Tereese. I liked her name, which sounded like Ms. Treat. I liked how I was able to walk right into her smile when she said "Hello, good morning." Her voice made me think of the cooing of our pigeons.

But one day, while standing in line to return to class from recess, another little boy punched me. Being a natural little boy, I punched him back. Games among little boys often start from punching and both our punches would have soon been forgotten, leaving no scars. But when I punched the other boy back, Ms. Tereese slapped me. With all her 20/20 vision, apparently she hadn't seen the first punch and that I had only defended myself. The slap was not that bad, but the pain in my heart hurt a great deal and served as an awakening. I didn't understand why I had a swollen face and not the other boy, too.

In first grade, Miss Rude slapped my hands a few times with a ruler and introduced my behind to the pine. From then on in school, I knew there was no justice, or if there was, it was selective. My second grade teacher, the white Mr. Williams, confirmed this. At times it seemed like every day I was getting paddled. I often wondered was it the way I looked, walked, or didn't talk? Or was there a neon sign on my butt which read, "Swat me if you are bored or have energy to expend"? Did all the teachers go off to lunch each day and decide who would guide the pine?

I still tried to learn, dabbling with printing and cursive writing. But the abuse picked up. After the paddlings in second grade from the white Mr. Williams, I went on to more of the same from the black Mr. Williams in third grade. It was equal opportunity paddling on me back in those days of the Civil Rights Movement. From then on, learning something proper and real was out of the question.

Even the principal, Mr. Chavez, got into the show. One day, in the hallway, he pulled me to the side and said, "Boy, you will never graduate from high school." I looked at him and wondered why he told me that. I did not know what graduate meant and what it had to do with high school, a place I had never even seen. But the words shot a hole in my already weak self-esteem.

The white Mr. Williams seemed to follow me from grade to grade. I remember him breaking two or three paddles on my butt in one session because I refused to cry. My ass must have built up calluses and my mind unwavering anger, pride, and strength. Mr. Williams swatted me so long one day, he seemed to cry from exhaustion.

One beautiful late spring day during recess on the playground, stretching my neck like a giraffe, I saw the white Mr. Williams go into the dark basement storage room under the auditorium near the outside ramp that led down from the cafeteria. We were playing four square—Andrew, Willie, Randy, Felix, and Clyde. My friend, Isaac and his neighbor, Gloria, along with other kids, hung on the fringe of the game waiting their turn to play.

Andrew stood next to me. I pointed to Mr. Williams who had unlocked the basement door and left the lock on the hinge.

"So?" said Andrew.

"I'll close the door on him."

"I dare you. You are not that crazy."

"You're not doing nothing!" said Willie.

"I'll lock his ass in there!"

"I bet you won't."

"A peanut patty."

"I'll do it for nothing!"

I slapped the rubber four square ball away and strolled across the playground. It was a warm day and I could smell the hot lunch simmering from the cafeteria and knew it was beef tacos and corn. I licked my lips like a young lion club sniffing meat. I could hear the leaves breathe softly in the desert heat.

As I walked, I sensed that Andrew, Willie, Randy, and Clyde were in tow. Then I saw Isaac and Gloria. Gloria was the prettiest and most athletic girl in school. She ran faster than most boys and beat a lot of us in tetherball. I joined the Christmas choir in the third grade just to stand near Gloria. I don't know if she even saw me.

Somehow word had flown around the yard that something was going down. The word spread like maggots on a wound. All the Crooks Street boys crowded in behind me as we moved across the marble-shooting dirt area, under a big maple tree, near the large windows of the first and second grade classrooms. We swept down the tetherball circle and then rumbled through the kickball arena and all the players joined in the march. The girls jumping rope and playing jacks under two shade trees bounded up and fell in stride. All the kids stood a few meters behind me. I did not look back until after I slammed the open twin door of the basement shut and locked it.

Mouths opened wide and eyes were as big as king-sized marbles. There were deep sighs, whispers, laughs, and ahs. Some of the kids scrambled away and others stood in silence for a long time. I felt neither joy or sadness at first, and then some kind of shift and hardness in my heart. Gloria did not say anything to me that day, but I saw her young cheetah-like smile. Mr. Williams started banging on the door, crying out to be released, yelling and whelping like a puppy. He had a fear of darkness and closed-in spaces.

A yard monitor finally contacted the principal, who released Mr. Williams. He was all red, sweaty, and frightened—like a kangaroo rat that had narrowly escaped a coyote. For the first time, Mr. Williams came out of the basement as a human being. Such a heart-warming feeling!

I was so pleased with the moment, I threw the yard monitor a finger. The principal and a couple of teachers had a paddling party on my behind. I stopped counting at twenty swats. Both Mr. Williamses were there. Yet, still, there were no tears. If the school had only known to tell my mom and dad, the whipping I would have received at home—one with a water hose, tree branch, or extension cord—would have brought streams of tears even from Samson.

Paddling parties were what school meant to me, so when Judith announced that she had been given permission to meet individually with students, and that the first consultation would be with me, I was jazzed and also anxious. What would it be to meet alone with a teacher without negativity, hostility, or abuse? With no slapping, paddling, hitting, or put downs?

Judith and I have never talked one-on-one, never shared a real conversation. She has not seen any of my writing except for one or two tiny jottings, nor have I asked any questions in class. I don't know what to expect; Judith and I might end up watching walls for an hour or so. Still, I look forward to this meeting as a skinny honeybee looks forward to spring.

Judith is surprised when, after she complains about the heat, I say, "Ninety degrees hotter, I'd be warm." She asks where I grew up. I have no idea where this question-and-answer time will lead. But I feel open and without any blocks. Judith must be shocked, as words flow freely from me.

We walk into the education building and pass the small guard station with the huge window that overlooks the prison's lower yard. We descend to the bottom floor, the one called the dungeon floor because at the end of the hall is a banned, barred door that leads to very old red brick chambers. One can look through the door and see the clasps and shackles that once chained prisoners to the walls.

When we make it to the classroom, I note that Judith jots down all I tell her about the heart of the high desert, Crooks Street, the heat, the red clay mountains that appeared to be my whole world, and the desert wildflowers after a rainfall. I think: Wow! Who is this educator, this poet, writing down something I say? She isn't writing a bad report. She isn't being an authority figure trying to put me down.

I brought with me bits and pieces, thoughts and feelings, that I'd written during the poetry classes. These jottings were inspired by class discussions, model poems, visiting guest artists, and fellow students, as well as by some book I had read while I sat out in front of the prison chapels overlooking the garden plaza, the only place in San Quentin where trees, flowers, and grasses grew and where butterflies, sparrows, and other small creatures hung out. The class enabled me to bring together and understand the subjects, philosophies, and wise sayings I had been studying for nearly ten years, gave me a way, even in my silence, to link and express ideas, vibes, thoughts, and feelings in my own way.

Sitting in the dungeon room, I see the interested smile on Judith's face and the curious flow of her voice that seem to welcome the words I have to say and the bits and pieces of writing I show her. There is a lot going on inside me, like the underground waters in the dry Mohave River that no one could see.

During all of my years in school and on the streets, I never went inside myself. Even now, in this classroom with Judith—my first positive exchange with a teacher—I do not believe my writing is poetry, or even complete sentences. On this hot September afternoon, I still do not believe that anything written by me is worthy, or that anything inside me is beautiful.

3

Mirrors

I N MY FAMILY, September was apples and honey, the start of the new year. Rosh Hashanah, followed ten days later by Yom Kippur. Holy days which I remember mostly as walking the blocks from my grandparents' house to the synagogue on Fairfax. Los Angeles was hot, red at the edges, windy and dry. I walked home with my mother and aunts. The men were still *davening* at *shul;* the women left early to get food onto the table by sundown. My aunts talked: Aunt Nora was learning to drive, there would soon be a sale at Bullocks. The sound of their words was one song, the crunch of fallen sycamore leaves under my shoes was another.

Around the mahogany table, in the evening, sat my *bubbe* and *zadie;* my mother; my great-aunts, Ida, Riva and Sadie; aunts, uncles, and cousins from all over L.A. My father. The babies—my sister, Debbie, and cousin, Beth—sat in high chairs. Even without the family in St. Louis and Detroit, every leaf was added to the dining room table. Uncle Aaron, stuck at this table's foot, sat almost into the hallway. *Abie, Izzie, Moishe, Zelig, Icki, 'Fraim.* Aunty Emma was the oldest of my mother's siblings, and when they were children in Detroit, she rounded them up at supper time by singing their names.

The first September I remember is before these Septembers. September 1949, and I'm not at my grandparents', but five houses north, 1322 Ridgley Drive, the house my father, mother, and I are about to move into. What I see when I remember is my father dismantling a crib in the corner of

Judith (age four, leaning on table) with her grandparents,
Aunt Nora, and a few of her cousins.

a small bedroom and light pouring through two south-facing windows. September light, red and gold, low light that steeps more than blazes. My father is bent to his task and he's talking to me. I don't remember his words but know he's telling me that the baby my mother has been carrying was born dead; he's telling me there is no more baby.

I remember a whoosh, almost like the light from the windows entering my body. A whoosh that fills me or wakes me or somehow lets me know I have skin and that this skin contains me. I—the one everyone calls Judy—is suddenly on one side of this skin and everything on the other side is not me, not Judy. I must not have known this before, though I don't remember what I did know. Before, was Judy not distinct from wallpaper, wood floor, double-hung windows, Daddy Bob, kewpie doll, Bubbe? I don't know, but with that whoosh I was separate. My father was across the room, the closet door was behind me, a tall tree stood outside the west window, and my brother was dead.

My mother came home from the hospital, we moved into our new house, my father was gone all day teaching. And? And where was this baby, this brother? No one mentioned him to me again. I felt restless, so suddenly a self, so suddenly separate. Something hovered. Light? A whisper? My father's words still in the bedroom? My brother? Wasn't any adult going to provide that barely-born spirit a place he could settle? Apparently not.

So I did. I scooped my brother into my heart and made him a home.

I don't remember my brother inside me, don't remember if his presence was a weight or more like a tickle. Did we speak? Was I sad, or did his presence make me feel less alone? Was he the one I would soon call Stony. *Don't sit down! Stony's right there on the couch.* Or: *Wait. Stony's still climbing the stairs.* Did my dead brother's spirit shape itself into Stony, the being others labeled "Judy's imaginary friend"?

I lay awake most nights in that small bedroom where my father had dismantled the crib, too frightened to close my eyes. There were monsters in the closet, that was for sure. The searchlight whose source my father explained so precisely was really, I knew, no matter my father's logic, a trail for witches. I could hear them cackle and call. Monsters, witches, and bombs likely to fall on the roof of our house. *La la la la* I tried to sing to myself in a you-can't-get-me pretend bravado. Or I told myself stories: I was the Lone Ranger's girlfriend; I played Sparky's magic piano as in the new record my mother had recently bought me. *Conjure the sound of the Lone Ranger's boots on gravel,* I didn't tell myself but must have somehow enjoined. *Conjure Sparky's red hair, hair like Cliffy's, our carrot-topped neighbor. Imagine yourself into a whole other world and maybe you will be safe.*

Fear lived in my legs, my feet, in the big brown shoes I wore that covered even my ankles. Fear in the trouble my feet had simply resting on ground. Fear lived in the device the doctor gave my mother to correct my turned-in hips. I placed my feet in this contraption at night, then lay on my back unable to move. I was a good girl—everyone said so—*reasonable,* so the panicked scream ready to burst buried itself instead in my throat.

My own favorite made-up story had me lost in a forest. I was cold, so cold. I threw off my actual blanket—thin, white cotton, flowers in quilted squares, bordered with brown scallops—to make nearly real the arctic I summoned. I imagined a bleak, stormy wind. I'd been lost for days. No food. Probably rain. When I was so cold I couldn't get any colder, I heard a sound in the stillness. Footsteps on leaves. A stranger appeared. He wrapped me in blankets and walked with my body held in his arms. I shivered, but he kept on in the dark. I imagined each moment of our walk for as long as I could, drawing it out. I felt so safe against this big body. Eventually we wound up inside a hut that was warmed by a fire. Somewhere I'd never been before. The stranger called the place home.

I told myself stories and taught myself to read stories in books, like the Golden Book I was allowed to buy each week at the supermarket as my parents shopped for groceries: *Pantaloon, Nurse Nancy, Doctor Dan the Bandage Man*. My mother read me longer stories in installments—*B is for Betsy, The Wizard of Oz, K'tonton*.

My father told stories from the floor where he lay prone between Debbie's bed and my own. Daddy Bob had three on-going series. Hal Stories featured a young, studious boy, a good boy, as my father was himself told always to be. Zillie was a pluckier hero, a courageous girl who, with a pinch of salt, became invisible and, with the tiniest taste of sugar, could fly.

The series I loved most was the one my father called Bob and Emma Stories. These were about my father's childhood first in Cripple Creek, Colorado, and then in Santa Ana, California. Emma, his older sister, got marquee billing, but most of the stories were about Bob, or *Robert* as he was called as a child.

For example: Five year old Robert begged and begged his mother for a donkey. Grandma Nettie resisted; Robert persisted. Finally his mother borrowed a neighbor's donkey for an afternoon and Robert was joyous. But no sooner had the boy been lifted onto the animal's back than the donkey bucked. My father tumbled, hit his head on a rock. Grandma Nettie wrung her hands, *I knew it. I knew this would happen, I knew it.*

Or: Mr. Dewar owned the general store in Cripple Creek, and he taught young Robert to sing "Just a Wee Doch an Dorus" as the Scotsman Harry Lauder sung the song. Mr. Dewar offered Robert a deal. Sing the song for customers and earn a handful of cookies.

Sometimes my father paused in his telling. The pause lengthened, grew into silence, and finally we heard a slight snore. Debbie and I rolled to our sides, looked down from our beds, and found our father asleep on the floor. Other times the telephone rang in the kitchen, and my mother came to our bedroom door to announce a colleague or student from UCLA on the line. My father most often took the call, and Debbie and I were left with a half-told story, having to find our own way toward sleep.

Aunty Riva also told stories. When she was a young girl in Russia, she came down with bronchitis every winter. Her father saved money

Judith (age seven) with sister Debbie   FAMILY ALBUM

and the year she turned sixteen, he planned to send her to the Riviera through the cold season. The doctor shook his head. *This girl won't live another winter, why bother with her?* Aunty Riva laughed when she told that story, for here she was, in her late sixties, a survivor of dozens of winters. A survivor of worse.

Aunty Riva told stories of escaping Russia just after the revolution; of tutoring the niece and nephew of the grand duke of Finland; of years in the ex-pat community in Berlin; of putting an ad in the *Jewish Daily Forward* trying to locate my grandmother in America; of making it to this country at the last possible minute, barely escaping Hitler. In Los Angeles, Aunty Riva, delicate and speaking perfect French, transformed herself from Riva Velinsky into Vera Villard. Madame Villard taught French to Beverly Hills matrons; Madame Villard was governess to Judy McHugh, Eddie Cantor's granddaughter.

When she visited from Detroit, Aunty Emma also told stories. She was the only one of my grandparents' children born in Russia, and she arrived on the boat with my *bubbe* in 1907. That boat landed in Boston on the fourth of July. When my grandmother saw the firecrackers exploding, she cried out—my Aunty Emma reported—"They have pogroms in America, too?"

My world was my mother's family, and the Lazaroffs didn't need to tell every story out loud to convey what they wanted to teach me. For there I was, kneeling on the kitchen chair, rolling dough into plump cylinders along with Bubbe as we baked coffee cake in her kitchen. There I was, staring at the photo in my grandparents' bedroom of Aunty Emma in her UNRA uniform on her way to the Displaced Persons camps after World War II to sing "Ani Mamin" to the survivors.

On Purim, Bubbe assembled baskets of fruit and baked goods and handed them to me. *Shalach Manos*, Bubbe said, and not much else. She never used the word "poor," or explained the requirement to help those in need. Bubbe just took my hand as we delivered one basket to the old woman on the second floor in the back of the apartment house two doors down and another to the recently widowed mother around the corner on Packard. I don't remember her words, but somehow Bubbe let me know being poor was not a fault, and that the Purim gift was ours—hers and mine. I was shy and afraid, knocking on the doors of people I didn't know, but I also felt something like pleasure or pride, as though my *bubbe* had chosen me to help right the scales of justice.

If some barking dog chased me as I walked up Ridgley Drive on my way home from school, if some neighborhood boys teased me about a bomb about to fall only on my side of the street, there was my grandparents' front door—five houses closer than my own—on which I could knock. I knew that front door would open and whoever stood there would welcome me in. Bubbe would say something in Yiddish to Zadie, and though he would sigh, he'd put on his jacket, take my hand, and walk me the rest of the way home.

My father's family—the Tannenbaums and Porgeses—lived nowhere near Ridgley Drive. Daddy Bob's parents, Henry and Nettie, died before I was born; my great-aunts lived in Denver. When a young woman, Aunt Irene taught in small Rocky Mountain towns. She boarded with a student's family, she told us, and rode to school side-saddle. Though Jewish, too, there was no *Judeleh* out of her mouth, no *shaine maidel*. Aunt Irene addressed each one of us as "dearie."

My father's sister Emma—I called her Ahmee—lived with her family in Glendale. The Elconins seemed exotic, Glendale not Jewish at all. Brockmont Drive, a winding road that climbed along a steep hillside, looked nothing like my neighborhood of square streets: Hauser, Curson, Spaulding. No sidewalks in Glendale. No Pico, the big boulevard at the end of my block, crowded with shops. Where were the delis like Joe and Ann's, the kosher butchers, banks, and beauty shops? Where was the five-and-dime filled with comic books and cherry phosphates?

Often we four Tannenbaums met the Elconins at El Cholo on Western. Enchiladas, not brisket. Tortillas, not chicken soup.

"Who was Jesus?" I asked.

"A man. A very good man," my mother responded.

"Oh little town of Bethlehem," I sang after learning the carol in school.

"A beautiful song," said my mother. "But maybe don't sing it for Zadie."

A story my father didn't tell us until we were older was the one in which he was chased up a tree by Santa Ana school kids yelling "Jew Boy" and "kike." Grandpa Henry came out of the house for the sake of his son, but the man was no match for the taunting children. My Lazaroff uncles walked the streets of Detroit ready to use their fists if need be, but my father's solution to ugly hurled words was to become the smartest, the best, the top of his class. In a letter he wasn't meant to see, a junior college professor wrote a glowing recommendation to the admissions department at the University of Chicago: *Robert isn't like the rest of his tribe.*

"Well, I'll be an African Gazoop," my father said when surprised by some news. Imagined animals with strange made-up names, puns, and jokes: my father liked being funny. He chomped down on a pretend cigar and wiggled his eyebrows, playing Groucho Marx at my seventh birthday party. "Say the secret word and win a hundred dollars," Daddy Bob imitated Groucho's Brooklyn accent.

Many bedtimes, my mother sang *Ai loo loo loo* or *lullaby and goodnight, with roses bedight.* The song I loved most, though, was neither Yiddish scat nor Brahms. *I've got shoes, you've got shoes, all God's children got shoes.* I tried to parse the meaning of *Everybody talkin' 'bout heaven ain't goin' there,* understanding that not everybody talkin' was goin', but not about irony and the frequent disconnect between words and action.

I wanted to trust that people meant what they said. So when, for example, Bubbe and I were at Aunt Annette's and my cousin Beryl pointed to the clock as we readied to leave and whispered, "Prisoners escape at 5:00 every evening. They gather in the tunnel under Pico. You'd better hurry,"

I believed her. I urged Bubbe to walk faster so we could make it through the pedestrian tunnel before the prisoners arrived. I even told her the reason. But Bubbe just smiled and continued her slow pace. I respected Bubbe. But my grandmother wasn't from this country and I figured Beryl probably knew more about prisoners and tunnels than did Bubbe.

Beryl again. We sat side by side in the breakfast nook at my house, and Beryl—five years my senior—took on the big-sister task of getting me, the pickiest of eaters, to finish my lunch. She used logic, warnings, and threats. And then I heard a rhythmic pounding from under the table. I could see Beryl's thighs rise and fall. Even so, when she said, "The sheriff is coming, the sheriff is coming. Can't you hear his horse getting close? Better eat all your food fast or the sheriff will get you," I believed her.

Why would Beryl lie? Why would anyone lie?

As much as I wanted to trust, I often sensed a chasm between sincere explanation and some truth I couldn't see but did perceive. My fears lived in this gap. When my father explained about that machine many blocks south whose light swept the sky through my bedroom window, I knew he was telling the truth. But I knew, too, that the searchlight was a path witches traveled to reach me. When my mother told me that the neighbor-hood boys were teasing about a bomb falling on our house and no other, I understood what she said, but the boys were insistent, and who could be sure a bomb wouldn't choose the home of the family whose name ended in *baum?*

I spent a great deal of time scanning the terrain between what appeared on the surface and what lurked underneath. The surface: my family, our clean kitchen, the smell of coffee cake baking, "Your Show of Shows" Saturday nights on TV. Underneath: witches, bombs, the buzzing fear in my skull.

How much of those years was spent inside on couches or chairs! Those inside spaces were actual rooms that I walked through, and they also occupied my imagination. The Aunties' apartment—with its interior staircase, its covered porch over the street—provided the layout I most often summon when an apartment appears in a novel I'm reading. Fifty-five years later and I still catch the smells of that second-floor flat: apple kuchen, strudel, and old lady musk.

If a novel takes place in a house, I usually imagine our own home on Ridgley Drive. Whether the text describes one or not, I see a big front porch above a wide lawn that is edged by beds of pansies and stock. I see our entry hall with its love seat and the breakfast nook in our east-facing kitchen. My friend Lolly's apartment gave me the set for any story taking place in a railroad flat. If a dwelling is described as "art deco," the kitchen in Rosalind's apartment appears in my mind. A novel placed in the suburbs summons Uncle Aaron's house in the Valley. Sometimes the fish tank from Uncle Al's house on Citrus sneaks in, or the maple table in Aunt Nora's kitchen, or Bubbe's O'Keefe and Merritt stove, the place mats and tall tumblers at my friend Mary Jo's, the tiny cubes of ice cream Ahmee served for dessert.

I wasn't always inside, though. I climbed trees with Cliffy and Stanley, the twins next door, and played statues with Mary Jo on our lawn. I walked to the bus stop on Pico to meet Zadie, shopped for my mother at Joe and Ann's, and sat under the fig tree in my grandparents' yard making purses from the thick fallen leaves. I helped Zadie carry the trash to the incinerator out back and watched him fill the stone cave, set the fire, close the latch. Some Sundays, Daddy Bob took me to Beverly Land where I rode the horse named Patches. I loved the two trees that stood at the furthest edge of our back garden. Twinkle Twinkle, I named one; Lullaby and Good Night was the other.

Inside was best, though, sitting on the wooden bench of our breakfast nook dictating stories that my mother transcribed. At school, too, I liked most the big crayons and the large sheets of newsprint. Reading circle didn't make me nervous, and I didn't mind being quiet and paying attention when the teacher told us what to do. Outside was where kids taunted *Tannenbaum Atom Bomb Cannonbomb* and where I stood as far back as I could watching others play jacks and jump rope. Outside was trying to make myself invisible when partners were picked and teams chosen.

Anyway, I *liked* listening and staying quiet: teachers, parents, uncles, and aunts. I liked watching the adults at home gesture as they talked about Edward R. Murrow, loyalty oaths, McCarthy, and Stevenson. I loved listening to the music made by their voices and watching emotion play on the planes of their faces. Lazaroffs, Tannenbaums, Porgeses: As though I were in a ballroom whose walls were mirrors shining light in all directions. It wasn't *me* reflected, exactly, but some bright beauty, a multi-faceted flashing. Years later, when I heard Sweet Honey in the Rock sing Ysaye Barnwell's "There Were No Mirrors in My Nana's House" with its repeating line, *and the beauty that I saw in everything/was in her eyes,* I recalled my own family.

When, as a young mother volunteering in my daughter's kindergarten class, I began sharing poems in schools, I found that teaching allowed my eyes to mirror love, too. Not only to Sara, my daughter, but to children I didn't even know. By September 1986, when Spoon and I sat in one of San Quentin's basement classrooms talking about poems, this being-a-mirror had become a favorite aspect of teaching: reflecting to others their own joy, beauty, curiosity, excitement, and humor.

San Quentin and beauty, prison and joy. I'd only taught the class in which I'd met Spoon for a single year, but that was more than enough time to note the oddity of teaching poetry—with poetry's inherent invitation to open one's mind, heart, spirit, and senses—in the closed world of a maximum security prison. Sure, there were some guards who joked in a friendly fashion with the men in blue and a few administrators who spoke about inmates as human beings, but the institution—the five tiers of cells in each cellblock; the locks, keys, and cages; the rules and procedures—seemed designed to reflect one consistent image of people in prison: monsters capable only of evil.

But my students weren't monsters. Despite the fact that almost all of them had been convicted of murder, they weren't evil. They weren't ciphers, either—not generic "convicts" or "inmates." Angel, Coties, Elmo, Gabriel, Glenn, Richard, Smokey, Spoon—each man had a name, each was a human being with his own nature and experience.

Angel told us that his father was a newspaperman in the Chicano community around Bakersfield. Quick and wiry, Angel warned us about manipulation and an elite based on "material, power, and possession," a phrase he sputtered at least once each class session. My favorite of Angel's poems demanded, "Who decides what a poem is?" letting us know "I am a poem/The world is a poem/The butterfly is a poem…/This poem is a poem/Speaking in tongues is a poem/A rock is a poem/Shit is a poem/And the corn in it too/is a poem."

Coties talked a lot about his children. He wrote them letters and called, but his family rarely had money for the long trip from Los Angeles so he did what he could at a distance to be the good father he wanted to be. Coties worried, not only about his own son and daughter, but about the community so many children like his own were growing up in. How had drugs become more important than black pride, Coties wondered. Coties let me know about anyone mentioned in the news doing good work, especially with youth. He told me to send these men and women poems from San Quentin; he told me to invite them all in to visit.

Elmo was the man guest artists commented on first as we walked away from the classroom, out the three gates, and down the long pathway back to our cars. "How can someone that smart be in prison?" most wondered. Elmo was not only smart, he could also talk with anyone, whether a fish (someone brand new to the prison), a professor, or a visiting poet. Elmo grew up black in a beach town north of Los Angeles, where he'd counted as friends thugs, hippies, low riders, and spiritual seekers. Elmo was editor of *The San Quentin News*, and both my strongest ally and biggest challenge. My ally because he went out of his way to teach me what he thought I needed to know about prison and because I could tell he looked out for me, even though I didn't really understand what such looking out involved. And my challenge because Elmo's sharp mind homed in on whatever seemed like a cover-up. Since childhood, I'd heard in my head what I called The Voice—a male drone that noted my every weakness, sloppily worded speech, or mixed motivation. Elmo noticed too, and always spoke out. I cared what Elmo thought and often over-reacted because his voice sounded so much like that of The Voice.

The mirrors of our classroom were poems read and written, visiting guest artists, conversations, laughter, and the human relationships we were building between us. In these mirrors Angel, Coties, Elmo, Spoon, and the others were not only prisoners, but also poets; not animals capable only of one worst act, but kind, funny, smart, generous, often sweet men. In San Quentin's world of concrete and hatred, our classroom was allowed to reflect light. I loved being in that room.

4

Nowhere But
Barstow and Prison

MY MOM AND DAD tried fifteen times to have a girl baby, but ended up with fifteen boys. We lived in a back house, just off Crooks Street, close to the dry river. A colorless, gray, two small-roomed, square, cement shack. One tiny bathroom and closet and another closet-sized impression of a kitchen. We bathed in an old round tin tub in bath water that had been boiled.

My dad worked for the Santa Fe Railroad. He and my mom came from Texarkana, Texas and Texarkana, Arkansas. My dad left the South first, after he got into a conflict with a white man and punched him, which was a hanging event for a black man in the 1940s. So he left, traveling as far away as he could, landing in Barstow, California, in the Mojave Desert.

There were hardly any fences on the river bottom where we lived. The soft sands rolled under and past Blacks Bridge. Blacks Bridge was all steel with bolts like small biscuits. When I lay under the bridge, and a train ran across, I felt its power like a herd of elephants or bison stampeding across the sky. I watched the different shapes the train's shadows created on the white sands. Usually I wore no shoes so that I could feel the sands of the river as my feet sunk into them.

When I stepped out of our house on Crooks Street, the purple and red clay mountains that surrounded me seemed to hold the whole world. I thought that up must be the only way out, so I had a habit of walking with my head

Spoon (front row, in striped shirt) with his parents and brothers.   FAMILY ALBUM

held back, my eyes looking upward. I often ran into things: trees, doors, and fences. Still, I kept my head up. Somehow I knew the universe was limitless. I looked for hours into the sky while lying on a sand dune along the dry river bottom. I had a secret spot beside the river, and sometimes I would whistle and semi-wild dogs would come running from all directions. When all the stars were out, I felt there was something hidden behind each one, as if the stars played hide-and-seek, off and on, like fireflies.

Whenever I saw a rainbow strung across the sky from B Hill to the mountains, I thought of a series of brilliantly colored sidewalks, each one leading into a new adventure, each one having its own mystery. Other times, I saw the rainbow as a gateway into a dream, a new dimension, something everlasting. Life seemed to go on forever. The stars, like the semi-wild dogs, were loyal to themselves, and they always shone together, even on the darkest night.

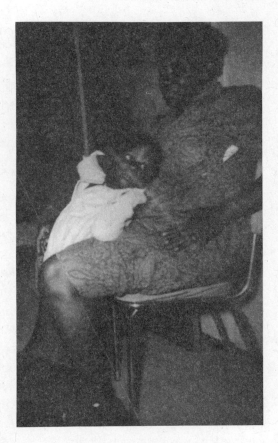

Spoon, age three. Little Stanley
and his mother, Hortense
Whitney Jackson.
FAMILY ALBUM

We had domestic animals on our land: chickens, rabbits, pigeons, tur-
keys, greyhounds, and hogs. I could sit for hours, for an entire day some-
times, watching them. Other times I crossed the dry river, a half-mile or so
from the back of our house, and watched the desert animals: road-runners,
lizards, rattlesnakes, jack and cottontail rabbits, and birds.

Yet I always longed to see more exotic creatures, the kinds I had read
about and had seen in picture books at school. I wanted to see pythons,
elephants, bears, whales, and zebras. I wanted to see the large birds of prey,
even vultures and buzzards. I wanted to see crocodiles and black panthers. I
wanted to see the big cats, the lions and tigers that inhabited far away places.

So I was very excited about my first field trip. The Parks and Recreation
Department ran a summer enrichment program to give children things to
do—sporting events and excursions. One trip was to the San Diego Zoo, and

I couldn't wait. The night before, I didn't get any sleep; I was up and dressed by three a.m., waiting.

We were to embark on this adventure from the Catholic school. Everyone gathered around the huge yellow school buses as we were loaded on to them. I ran to get a window seat so I could view the passing land as we traveled. I sat looking out of the window, thinking of all the animals I would get to see. Then another boy came and sat beside me. I wanted to be alone, in a seat to myself, to observe. So when the kid would not leave, I beat him up. Nothing bloody or long.

I was immediately kicked off the bus by one of the adults. As I stood there watching the yellow vehicles pull away from the sidewalk, one by one, a part of my heart pulled away with each bus. My heart dropped like a sparrow that had been shot. I sat down on the curb in the early morning sunshine and watched the wagons full of smiling children go on their way. I would have preferred a paddling instead of missing this field trip.

At least my mom and dad were not around, so they did not know the reason I was bounced off the bus. For the home beatings stung far worse than the paddlings I got at school. Sometimes my dad caught me with the extension cord in the bath tub. An extension cord on a wet, naked body stings like a whip. Dogs, cats, coyotes, and other howlers would have envied how loudly I bellowed. When the beating was over, my skin was afire, puffed up in places, as though lashed with a whip. Other times, when I thought I had gotten away with something, I lay sleeping in bed, on the floor, or on the couch, only to be awakened by a water hose, tree branch, or extension cord. The only safe place was my spot under the house, a place only dogs, snakes, and spiders lived. I never went that far under and I had to come out for food, school, church, and even—eventually—the whipping.

Unlike the beatings at school, though, my mom and dad beat me for a reason, when I knew myself that I had done something wrong or had broken a family rule or sin. I am sure my parents based their whippings on the Bible, some verse about sparing the rod. Although I had no concept of God, Jesus, or sin, I understood these whippings for stealing, staying out late, or sneaking out of church services.

People at school never spoke with me about why they paddled or slapped me. No one at school ever showed me they cared. Whereas after a beating at home, my mom was still there, breakfast and dinner still served. My mom never failed to accept me no matter what law of society I had broken. When

I got older, and the cops took me to the police station, my mom would pick me up as soon as she could, or she'd have the cops drop me off at home. Sure, I would get another whipping for truancy, or shoplifting, or whatever I'd done, but my mom and dad left no doubt that I was part of a family.

My hopes, my dreams, my desires—the whole world, everything around me—seemed violent: society, school, church, the pigeons, chickens, hogs, and dogs we raised at home. I stood at the pigeon coop and watched the birds battle over box houses, trying to peck each other's eyes and beaks out. They slapped each other upside the head with their wings and then turned around in a circle dance. The winner got the love and the female. When the dogs fought, especially the semi-wild ones, their fights were long, vicious, and sometimes to the death.

My father moved to California due to the racial violence of the time. My father hit my mom and they both hit me. I fought at school, fought with my brothers, and fought with Crooks Street friends. The teachers gave beatings. I broke my brother Jimmy's arm with a two-by-four when he threatened to take my money. My brother Jerry went off to war in Vietnam. My brother Arthur was scalded with hot water and stabbed by one of his many girlfriends. Even the *Wizard of Oz* was violence-filled.

Spoon (left, in cap), age eight,
with some of his brothers and River Bottom boys. FAMILY ALBUM

35

All of the whippings, at home and at school, only toughened my ass, my resolve, and my resentment. I grew numb. The beatings did not hurt anymore; they made me angry, empty, and sad and further reinforced my wayward ways. They showed me that power, pain, and perhaps even gain, were the way of things and the way of life. All of us tough guys, most of us from Crooks Street, hung out together, stealing and fighting each other and kicking the not-so-tough guys' asses, taking their lunches or lunch money. I felt nothing inside when we took from others. My sense of compassion was put to sleep, along with my desire to learn and to balance my darker side with my lighter side.

There were no hugs in my family that I can remember, no one ever said the words "I love you." Sometimes in the summer, though, my mom sat under a tree with me at her knees. She rubbed my head and thought of whatever it was she thought about on shady, warm days. These moments were blessed, even without the words "I love you." During the summer, she also gathered all of her ice cream making tools and sat on the porch, overlooking the field, the long bridge, the railroad station, and B Hill. No matter where I was, I would come out to be near her and to hang out with her. It seemed like whenever she cooked, snapped snap beans, or made ice cream, I would be the only one there, sharing a silence filled with the making of food. My mom put a little box of powder, some salt, and some ice around the churner. I loved watching her turn a magic wheel until everything thickened. At just the right moment, Mom would look away so that I could playfully sneak a taste.

My oldest brothers—ten to twenty years older than I—were like legends: heard about but rarely seen. My brother Rob was the Hercules of the family, big and muscle-bound like an alpha-male lion. Early Jr. sometimes backed his car onto our land and turned on his eight-track player, blasting Earth, Wind and Fire; Al Green; and Otis Redding. When I caught Rob or Early Jr. on pay day, they would give me some change, and I would run off to the River Bottom store for soda pop or peanut patties.

Another older brother, Jerry, left Crooks Street and became a soldier. When he came back from Vietnam, he dreaded his hair, took up with his old sweetheart, packed up all his belongings, and moved up to northern California. Brother Arthur was too cool. Bow-legged, pimped out, and laid back, Arthur was a player who lived off the ladies and eventually moved to the big city. Garland also went into the service and was stationed in Germany for a while before coming back home with a bunch of fancy musical

Spoon's brother, Rob, lifting hog for fun.

gadgets. Abe left to go to college in a place called Bakersfield. Not long after I broke Jimmy's arm, he became a self-made preacher. He hexed me. Terry, Bishop, and Garland were all still at the house, but I knew the rest of my brothers from the family portrait hanging next to the metal bird cage that had a yellow canary in it.

And there were also my three half-brothers and four half-sisters. Pops rolled around a lot. He never loved Mom, although she loved him and never took up with another man. When I saw my Pops out on the town with other women, he smiled as if he had hit a homerun with a corked bat. I would never tell my mom, though. Her already broken heart did not deserve the enhanced misery.

37

The summer before junior high blessed me with more height and bulk. So the first time I was sent to see the vice principal, I stepped into his office with my head up, my lips pushed together, my eyes squinting, ready to pounce, run, or hold my ground. Sure enough, there on the wall hung four long, thick wooden paddles; one had holes in it. The vice principal spoke from behind his desk, without looking up.

"Come in and close the door, Jackson." He played with some paperwork. I said nothing.

"I see you have been in some kind of trouble ever since you arrived here." Again I said nothing.

The vice principal came from behind his desk, rubbed his chin, eyed his paddles, and then looked back at me. He stood a few inches taller than I did.

He grabbed his famous paddle with holes in it and fondled it like he was trying to goose it.

I stood my ground with mad tears in my eyes. I said nothing, but my fists were coiled like rattlesnakes. The vice principal paused and then suspended me.

History, science, math, language: I could not absorb anything from my classes in junior high and believed that it was impossible to learn anything in school. I gave up, remaining silent in class and never raising my hand. I was a teenager, mad and disliking authority. Teachers understood that I would not accept any beatings without a fight. I was too big for whippings now—at school or at home.

By this time, my parents had separated. Despite everything else, each of my parents had a strong work ethic that they instilled in their boys. I loaded and hauled junk to junk yards, and with the Crooks Street boys, went up and down the long roads and highways collecting soda pop bottles to redeem. We sold *Desert Dispatch* newspapers for a dime on Main Street and at the railroad station.

But we also stole—soda pop bottles and items from unattended cars, rail cars, and trucks. Anything that had value and was not tied down, we sold to get dope and drinking money. I stole in the daylight on the way to school and at night in the darkness of the desert. I stole from anyone, even family and neighbors. I had no conscious idea of conscience, no sense that I hurt the people I stole from. I did have feelings, but they were aloneness, anger, and rage.

The deeper I got into my teen-age years, the more disillusioned and alone I became. I had always liked being alone, but now I thought I was supposed to be like everyone else. I never felt accepted by anyone during my teen-age years because I did not or could not accept myself. I had no idea who I was or what I was doing on this, or any, planet. I did not realize that the objects I stole could never fill the dark pit in my lost soul.

I often hung out with white friends, listening to the Rolling Stones and Jimi Hendrix; smoking weed; popping purple haze, orange sunshine, and window pane acid. I lived on the backside of life, caring about nothing but the next party. I knew I would not be able to make things work in regular high school, as I did not understand any teacher or subject. Besides, they kicked me out when I got in a fight with a white guy who'd just called me a nigger. I picked up a desk to smash him, but something stopped me. I did not quit school, though, because school is where I could find girls. Plus the words of my elementary school principal echoed in my soul. I could not let those words—"Boy, you'll never graduate from high school"—come true.

So I went to continuation high school, and though I learned nearly nothing, I did discover Jack London's books, *White Fang* and *The Call of the Wild*. These little books were the first, and only, ones I read in any school. I couldn't believe there were books about dogs, books I could read and understand.

That year was probably my best year. I had a series of jobs: temporary food service on the graveyard shift at Fort Irwin Military Base, a summer job working for CalTrans, and then a gig at Yellow Freight Trucking Company. I bought my first car even before receiving my license. In this small community, where I was expected to live my whole life, my car and good jobs were considered a success. The older folks sat on their stoops and porches praising, "Look at that Jackson boy." Inside, however, I was still a robot thinking I was a living being.

Despite Mr. Chavez's prediction, I did graduate from high school. I graduated without knowing how to build a complete sentence, without knowing how to do simple fractions, without knowing how to read beyond a sixth grade level, and without knowing how to communicate with my fellow human beings. I graduated without ceremony, but I was pleased to see the joy in my mom's face. A joy that was short lived.

Not long after graduation, I was on one of my runs. I got caught up, was shot, and then killed someone. The killing was not premeditated, but it was totally my fault. In the depth of my heart and soul, I felt that what I did was wrong. I did not set out to kill anyone that night, but the fact is I did. The night I was arrested, I saw in my heart and soul that my mom knew something big was wrong. I did not tell her what happened, but the silence that fell on the moment was sorrowful and life-changing.

I was supposed to come to prison. I deserved to do some time and make amends. I was ready to be judged and convicted for the killing I had done. But I did not expect the inherently racist judicial system that inflated my charges and determined my trial and conviction.

The day of my arrest, I had signed up with the Marines. I had just turned twenty and wanted to enlarge my world. Instead my world shrank to an isolated cell on the corner of the city jail. All I could do was to pace and to try to drown out the cheers I could hear from the football games at the high school near by.

During my trial, my mom and dad came to visit me. It was sad but good to see them together, in the same room, with a common goal and bond. I could see in their eyes that something had changed. This environment did not fit them any more than it suited cattle to live in trees. Perhaps it was the first time I had really looked at my parents. It was certainly the first time I recognized that no one could get me out of the trouble I was in now. There were no magic sidewalks in the sky over the purple and red clay mountains to lead me away from this mess I had created. This trouble made all the fights with my brothers, all the problems in school, and all the mean words irrelevant. This trouble left a cut, a big open wound, in our family. I could see in my parents' eyes that one of their own had fallen. My mom's eyes held a million words. My dad said one of longest sentences I'd ever heard him speak—"Boy, you better pray!"

And I did pray that night and for many nights after. Incarceration brought the fact that my parents truly did want the best for me into full bloom in my heart, mind, and soul. From then on, I never lost sight of this truth. We were family, and when one falls, the others are there to pick him up. Before, I could not see the family unity due to my own uselessness, ignorance, and lack of feeling. I could not feel the unity through the beatings, fights, and mean words. I could not see from the way my dad treated my mother—hitting and abusing her—how he cared for her, though he never loved her.

I sat across the table, looking at my parents who had come to this place that for them, as for me, was alien, dark, and one step away from hell. They could only reach out with their hearts and souls but this was enough. Now my own soul and heart had eyes to see and ears to hear my parents' silence. I realized that my mom had always told me things that could help me, and that, although my dad had rough ways and many women, he had never been in trouble with the law. He, too, had wanted the best for me. Both wanted me out of trouble, jail, and hell. Now I wondered, when I was young and my dad warned me to "never let darkness catch you not at home," did he mean only our home on Crooks Street, or perhaps home in other ways, too.

Now I could see and feel so clearly what it meant to be part of a family, to be part of Crooks Street and the River Bottom. I had new eyes, new ears, and mind. I knew now how, in one moment, life can change on you like a twister. I had been sleep-walking for twenty years and now I had awakened. But to what?

It was like I'd had blinders on during my first two decades on earth. My ears had earplugs. Even my heart was hidden. Hearing the guilty verdict, I felt disgust for the jury. Those twelve white folks were not my peers, did not know me, and had no human right to judge me. I felt that because my victim was white and my jury was all white, I had been railroaded. So I stood up and yelled out at them in court, calling them a bunch of racist white muthafuckers. At the same time, I heard my mom and aunt cry out in pain as the sheriffs rushed me to the floor and carried me out of the courtroom.

After they found me guilty of the murder, I awaited the sentencing of life without possibility of parole or death. The jury could not choose between the two, so the judge gave me life without parole. At twenty, one cannot grasp the depth of a no-parole life sentence. There is nothing to compare it to, other than death. At twenty, one does not think he will do a life sentence. A life sentence does not sink in immediately. It can take seven to ten years to begin to understand. Life without parole is too big to grasp, or come to grips with, in the moment.

I sat down to breakfast, my first morning in prison, in a dining hall stuffed with prisoners. The noise and the mood of the place was maddening, like stepping into a huge, dark cave full of hungry bats. I could not find any familiar spot inside of myself able to relate to the bars, concrete, steel, guns, and to the guards barking out orders to hurry and eat.

I was ignorant about all prison ways. I came from the desert, the natural world—purple and red clay mountains, open spaces—and there was nothing natural about cells. Even the air was tainted and twisted with unrealness, fleeting hope, and violent unrest. I was naïve and also unconnected to any inner spirit. But my will to survive took over. I learned quickly to keep my laughter, smiles, and feelings inside and hidden behind a mask. Silence and dead-eyed frowns kept the strangers and guards at bay.

Besides, what cause was there for smiles or laughter? I had killed someone. There was nothing to talk about and no one to talk to, no one to hold my hand, nothing to dream or hope for. Never had I been so alone in a crowd. I felt I walked among bodies in one dimension while I strolled in another.

What could I compare this new life to? Perhaps the flood control tunnels under the railroad station we roamed in as kids, the way those tunnels shrunk and grew darker and more suffocating the deeper we descended. Could I compare my life in prison to Campy, the greyhound that caught five rabbits, but died slowly at home under the shade tree never catching his breath? Or could I compare this existence to hiding under our green house? I watched everything then, a completely unseen little boy. As though I was invisible, which I wanted to be.

5

By Heart

O<small>N A TABLE</small> at the back of the classroom, I wrote the opening of what would become my first real story. I had just turned eleven, and this classroom was not in Los Angeles, but in Turin, Italy where my father had come to teach during his sabbatical year and where we lived for six months. Three teachers rotated among the fourth- through eighth-graders at Scuola Svizzera. Mrs. Rodoti taught us history, geography, science, and Italian. Miss Lutz taught us arithmetic. Or she did so when she wasn't crying. Miss Lutz cried often, running from the classroom to sob on the shoulder of Mrs. Lutz—our principal and Miss Lutz's mother. Miss Grimshaw was our English teacher and her curriculum included asking us to write stories. Her method of instruction was to put a series of phrases on the chalkboard: Rita Remembers, The Night of the Black Cat, The Shut Curtains. We students were each to choose one as title for a story we then had thirty minutes to write.

Stories, my favorite thing. Before I knew how to form letters, I dictated stories to my mother, and she wrote them down on the backs of the mimeographed course lists and research notes my father brought home from UCLA. My mother transcribed my words, and I drew accompanying pictures. Even at four, I found it funny: which were the front sides of these sheets, which the back, my illustrated story or those typed words from my father's university world far away from our house?

-and-pictures in the first grade, too. Mrs. Green printed words
lower case letters on large sheets of newsprint: jump, truck, dog.
placed these sheets on the wooden tables at which we children sat,
anded out boxes of thick crayons, and told us to read each word silently
and then to draw what that word described.

Letters—t r u c k—were lines on classroom paper and on pages in books.
Each shape had its own sound, sounds I recited along with everyone else
when Mrs. Green held up Ts, Cs, and Ks in front of the class. The shape of
words, though, not the sounds of letters, taught me to read on my own
before coming to school. I put no effort into this learning. I simply looked,
again and again, at the books I loved; listened and noted as my mother read;
and soon I knew every word of those stories. Words from *Doctor Dan the
Bandage Man* were also in *Pantaloon*. "Boy," "and," "black," "dog," "mother,"
"home." Reading meant words and the forward motion that linked them.
Words and forward motion, that's how stories were told.

Letters were symbols Mrs. Green urged us to *sound out*; words named
the world: boy, black, dog, mother, home; stories strung separate things to-
gether: the boy and his black dog ran home to mother. But letters, words,
and stories were empty, meant nothing, without my own imagination to
bring them to life. When my mother read me stories in books, I, of course,
imagined the scenes she described. When I dictated a story, Mama wrote
down the words leaving plenty of room for the pictures I'd draw. When
Mrs. Green gave us first graders sheets of newsprint marked t r u c k, I
paused for a moment, visualized *truck*, and then drew one. When I read
books on my own, I could see—in my mind's eye, as the phrase accurately
has it—the heroine's red hair and blue dungarees; the sun-filled kitchen
with a mom at the sink; a schoolyard, a park, the grandfather's barn. I
could see the new puppy and naughty kitten, as well as the flowers and
trees lining neighborhood streets.

On this February afternoon at Scuola Svizzera, I waited in a state of alert
anticipation as Miss Grimshaw wrote each phrase on the chalkboard. Then
I picked up my pencil and copied the words, "A Girl with a Dream." My
eyes remained open, but their focus shifted from the classroom I sat in to
the story I was about to discover. For discovery is how I experienced stories.
Whether listening to a tale Daddy Bob told, Mama read from a book, or
reading the story myself once I could read, my listening ears and moving
eyes triggered whatever it was in my brain that made pictures. And some-

44

how those pictures linked and leapt so that *this*, and *this*, and finally *this* did not seem isolated moments but a flow, a progression, a *story*. Hunger to discover how *this*, and *this*, and *this* added up made me a reader. And now Miss Grimshaw and her title ideas made me hungry to write. The process of discovery was nearly the same, only reversed. Instead of words leading to pictures, now the pictures in my mind lead to words I put on paper.

Because of Miss Grimshaw, I began paying conscious attention to these pictures and how to court them. The process involved looking, of course, but not at what was in front of my eyes: not at my desk, the chalkboard or the apartment across the street from our school. I *could* have looked at that apartment which belonged, the eighth graders told us, to the man who owned Fiat and, *look*, the drapes have been drawn for two weeks now. Something's wrong, something's fishy, maybe he murdered his wife, or no, maybe he himself has been murdered.

If I'd chosen "The Shut Curtains" as title, I could have written that story, the one a half-dozen of us imagined together as we stared out at the apartment across from the school at break time. But I'd chosen "A Girl with a Dream" and most of me was already elsewhere, not in Scuola Svizzera, but back in Madrid where my family had spent four or five days when we arrived in Europe a few weeks before.

Sitting in my classroom chair in Torino, I saw the portrait of Franco that hung in every Madrid restaurant we ate in, every shop, every museum; the small towns we drove through on our way to El Escorial and Toledo; the children in the dirt roads of these towns, their bare feet and ragged clothes. I heard my father's long answer when I asked why, though it was a week day, the children weren't in school. I half-saw those sights, half-heard those sounds, even as I sat in Scuola Svizzera. I felt again the astonishment I'd felt on the road to Toledo: Lack of money keeps some children on the street instead of in school? Leaders don't care? In my mind's eye, I saw the woman I had wished, that afternoon in Spain, I could become. She was pert, with long auburn hair. I could see in the way she moved that she knew how to get things done and that she wouldn't take no for an answer. As I imagined this woman, I heard her name—Stevie, the name of the older sister of my friend, Candy Rollins. Stevie Rollins *was* pert; she had long auburn hair and seemed sure of herself. I knew I was too shy to grow into someone like her, but maybe I didn't need to—maybe I could write a story about her instead.

From Miss Grimshaw on, I knew I wanted to be a writer. When we returned to Los Angeles, I began writing a novel whose opening chapter took place at a cemetery in Ekaterinaslav where a character with my own *bubbe*'s story stood mourning the death of her mother. I kept on writing stories through my teen-age years, and the characters in these tales accompanied me as I climbed the stairs of John Burroughs Junior High, or took the gym bag from my locker at Grant High School. These characters let me know who they were, their natures, motivations, and values. *What would she do if…? What will he say when…?* I didn't shout out to passing students *don't step on him*—as I had long ago with Stony—but I was as curious about these characters and their needs as I had been about that earlier "imaginary friend."

Decades after my teen-age years, I'd ask the first and second graders with whom I shared writing to tell me about imagination. *Like dreams, but you're not sleeping. Like a movie inside your head. You can make up something not real and pretend that it's real.* Real/not real were words always used.

So I devised a game. *In your imagination,* I directed the little ones, *see yourself outside on a very hot day.* I asked them to notice what they were wearing. Green pants? Purple shirt? I asked them to feel the sweat running down their sides. *Now you hear something. What is it? A bird? Maybe the tune of the ice cream truck.* I took the children on a journey that ended up where they lived, with someone they love—maybe their mother, maybe their grandfather or a neighbor—in the kitchen, making the child's favorite food. *Now you're sitting at the table and this person you love is putting your favorite food in front of you. Can you smell it? Does it smell yummy? Notice the taste on your tongue and the sensation as the food goes down your throat. And what about the feeling in your heart? How does your heart feel, eating your favorite food, made for you by someone you love who you know loves you?*

When the imagining was over, almost everyone wiggled his or her hand in the air, wanting to tell us all what they'd seen. *Okay,* I'd say, *Imagination might not be real in the way the chair I'm sitting in is real*—I'd thump the wood, a sound we could hear with our ears—*but imagination's some kind of real because you all can tell me what happened even though your actual body never left this room.*

I'd asked the children to *see* what they were wearing, to *hear* the bird or ice cream truck, to *feel* the sweat run down their sides. Writers need their senses, I told the little ones: sight, smell, taste, touch, and hearing.

Of course, well-developed sensitivity often tends toward hypersensitivity, a condition artists are prone to and one that frequently left me bombarded by what my senses perceived; I was assaulted by the roar of a motorcycle, overwhelmed by the taste of chocolate, pummeled by the smell of soft boiled eggs, done in by the lushness of a thick swath of red paint. Which is why my father sometimes accused me of being like the princess who tossed and turned in the Hans Christian Anderson story, unable to sleep due to the tiny pea placed underneath twenty eider-down quilts, themselves resting on twenty mattresses. *Her* hypersensitivity proved to the prince and his mother that this young woman was, indeed, a real princess. *My* hypersensitivity made me nervous (and led to my father's annoyance).

I don't know about real princesses or other artists, but I survived my hypersensitivity by inventing stories. There was a girl in my story and each morning she readied herself for school. She played Four Square at recess when she had to, or Dodge Ball. I didn't have to be afraid; this Judy doing long division and taking spelling tests was only a character in a book I composed. The story-girl brought permission notes from her mother allowing lunch at Town & Country, the open-air shopping plaza next to the school. She ate spaghetti with friends, drank chocolate cokes. This girl played on the porch with Cathy and Carol from the duplex next door. She roller-skated around the block. She was a normal girl having fun. No one knew that girl wasn't me.

Later, too, it wasn't me trying to make my way down John Burroughs Junior High's central staircase. No, I was throwing coins in the Trevi Fountain and making a secret wish that was sure to come true. It might look like I was being jostled in Grant High School's crowded hallways, but really I was walking arm in arm with my handsome lover along La Promenade des Anglais in Nice.

What I told the children is true—we artists need our senses and imagination. But true, too, is what I didn't tell them: hypersensitivity and an overactive imagination can lead one—as they led me just after I started college—to blurred borders in the real/not real department. Even at that time, 1964, before the days of biochemical descriptions and pharmacological responses, doctors were ready with labels and pills. None of which fit or helped.

What helped first was, dance. For I found there was no way to manage a *grande jette*, stretches, or rib isolations without inhabiting my body.

47

Hypersensitivity and an imagination-run-amuck had metaphorically frozen my muscles; leaping across a studio floor reminded me that I could move.

Honestly, though, even before what the doctors called my breakdown, I hadn't much lived inside my own skin. I'd wanted to be a writer, yes, and I was good at imagining, but there was another aptitude required, and this one I hadn't yet discovered or been taught. A writer needs eyes able simply to rest on a face, object, or scene; needs ears to catch not only words spoken, but also timbre and tone. Such attention arises from the body, not from a racing mind that aches to escape into an imaginary world.

I met Ronnie when I was eighteen and what helped next was love. Riding down Wilshire in his Corvair convertible, warm wind soft on my skin; walking along the beach in Santa Monica, holding hands as we talked; laughing at the Calder mobiles as we explored the newly opened Los Angeles County Museum of Art; mornings, afternoons, and evenings making love: I began to learn the pleasures of settling into my body and getting to know another person intimately, through every sense.

Ronnie gave me Lawrence Durrell's *Alexandria Quartet* to read, and over ice cream at Blum's, we talked about Justine and Clea as though these characters were among our best friends. At McCabe's, we listened to Elizabeth Cotton and Mississippi John Hurt; we watched *Jules and Jim* in a small theater on La Brea and *8½* at UCLA. We saw *La Strada* at the Tantamount Theater in Carmel Valley on our first driving trip north. I'd read books my whole life; I'd listened to music. Dostoevsky, Herman Hesse, Bob Dylan. I'd already learned from so many, already signed up for life as an artist. And now Ronnie introduced me to Giacometti and Leonard Baskin, Guiletta Massina and Jeanne Moreau, Fellini and Truffaut. Ronnie and I met in the summer of 1965, rented an apartment together that fall, and lived on the Venice/Santa Monica border for four months. June, 1965 to the following January, a mere half-year, and yet so much of my being, as a woman and artist, was shaped by that time.

I was still eighteen when Ronnie and I moved to Berkeley, nineteen when we married, and twenty-three when our daughter was born. I pushed her buggy over the sidewalks of our neighborhood in the summer of 1970 and Ronnie asked, "Do you know why I call Sara, The Moon?"

I guessed, but each guess was wrong.

"She's not our son," he explained. "She's our moon."

Judith, her husband Ronnie,
and their daughter Sara,
1971.   FAMILY ALBUM

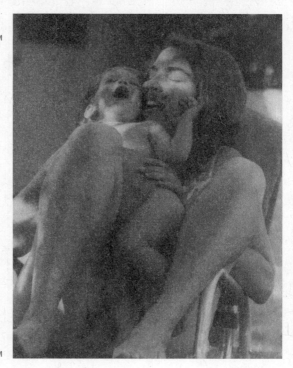

Judith and Sara, singing,
1971.   FAMILY ALBUM

When Sara was eighteen months old, I began writing a book. About imagination, actually, about women's dreams, fantasies, and journals. I wrote during playgroup mornings and my daughter's nap time. I wrote whenever I could. One afternoon, almost two years after I'd begun the project, I tucked Sara into her bed and my little girl said, "You can go write your book now."

"Guess what, Moon?" I'm sure I was smiling. "I finished the book."

"Well," Sara said without pause, "write another one!"

Writing another one was my intention. Before I could, though, we moved from Berkeley to southern Mendocino County, one-quarter mile from the ocean. Ronnie and I wanted a life where we had plenty of time to make furniture (him) and to write (me). But first we had to build the small house we would live in. Hammering nails, raising walls, and cooking dinner back at the campsite where we'd pitched a tent while we built our house, left no time or focus for "writing another one" or for writing long prose at all.

So, although I'd never done so before, I began writing poems. I hadn't read many or written any, but my good friend Gail Todd—we met when our daughters were babies—was a poet and her work attracted me to the form. My first poems were like stories. Sara was in them, and Ronnie. I wrote poems to my father the professor, to my mother and sister. Zadie appeared in a poem, his gnarly hand extended, its fingernail still ripped and gone. He led me toward death, a place where Bubbe still bustled, boiling water in the samovar to welcome me with a glass of hot tea.

Ronnie and I made the simple life we'd hoped for. We lived on very little money and had time to make furniture and write. Our little home was surrounded by tan oak, chinquapin, a few redwood. Through the trees, we could see the ocean downhill. I earned my share of the small income we needed by cleaning houses, doing some secretarial work, sharing poems with children in Sara's elementary school, and eventually teaching college extension classes in Point Arena, the town nearest our home. Some other parent or I took the children to swim in the Gualala River most summer days. In the winter, Ronnie and I kept the fire going in our Ashley wood stove and watched rain beat against our cabin's windows and skylight. We three were basically happy; our life was quite sweet.

And then, in the months before my thirty-third birthday, sweet soured for me. I began to feel trapped, though I recognized that the trap was one I had wanted, one I'd done all I could to create. Maybe I was due for the spiritual transition often associated with the age of Christ's death and resurrection. Perhaps I was having another breakdown. Could be I was just self-indulgent. In any case, I felt the need to go deeper, compelled to step onto a road I couldn't see but did sense. I could explain none of this to Ronnie who felt he'd be happy to live the rest of his life just as we were.

I was thirty-two, and then thirty-three. Ronnie was the only man I'd ever made a life with. I had no experience or skills to work with what I was feeling; the only solution I could see was to leave the marriage. So I sold the few items I owned, converted those two thousand dollars into travelers' checks, and flew off to Europe. There I wandered, took lovers, hitch-hiked, wrote poems, and prayed that whatever force I was following was for the good and not the work of the devil.

Three months into the journey, Sara joined me. We wandered together around London and Amsterdam, found a small room in Madame Seehausen's home in Paradou, and for a short while built a nest in this Provençal village. I cleaned house for a city councilman's family and Sara attended the town's two-room elementary school, stopping at the *boulangerie* on her way home to pick up a fresh baguette for our lunch. I walked to the *bureau de poste* to get the mail and to the Tuesday market on the town square to shop for cheese and vegetables, washed clothes in the bathtub, and kept food cool at night by setting it between our glass door and the outside shutters. I wrote funny poems for Sara along with drawings of made-up creatures. We explored back roads together, talking and looking.

"You're weird," Sara told me one day as we walked to see the traveling circus that had come to Mausanne, the next village over. "A good weird," she added.

I was glad that she thought so, hoped she was right.

My girl and I returned to Point Arena, and the summer before Sara began high school, moved back to Berkeley where rent for two bedrooms in a shared house was nearly twice the $300/month that had been our whole monthly budget in the country. I scrambled to piece together a living—workshops through California Poets in the Schools, research for a psychologist writing a book, organizing a resource library for the Berkeley school district. Before long, teaching at San Quentin each Monday night was one of the pieces.

And after the first year—with a grant from the California Arts Council—a larger piece, the main one. The individual consultation I held with

Spoon began this new phase. Now I not only taught the Monday night class but also offered additional classes; one-to-one teaching in the cell blocks; and learned from Jim Carlson, who ran the arts program at Quentin, how to prepare the memos and ducat lists required for my classes..

One afternoon, I walked into the education building, and Spoon appeared from some seeming nowhere. He quickly handed me a poem and then disappeared. I read the first stanza—

Restless, unable to sleep
Keys, bars, guns being racked
Year after year
Endless echoes
of steel kissing steel

—and read through to the end. A poem! Spoon's first real, no question about it, poem.

I loved Spoon's words, images, use of sound, and flow. But it wasn't only "No Beauty in Cell Bars" as a poem that caused me to cry that afternoon. No words attached to my emotions, but the words I'd use now are: I felt as though I was witnessing a birth. Elmo had come to our class already a writer and every one of my students had written at least one fine poem. But reading "No Beauty in Cell Bars" felt different from reading Angel's "What is a Poem?" or Coties's "Kickin' it with Loneliness," two poems I still use, more than twenty years after they were written, as model poems when teaching. Spoon's poem seemed not only the work of a poet who had developed enough craft to shape an inspiration, but also the expression of a man who'd discovered something important about himself.

After marriage and motherhood, bouts of mental distress, years of reading and writing, building a home, and adventures in Europe, I had some familiarity with recognizing one's path in life, summoning the courage to walk it, and maintaining enough heart to keep on, one foot after the other. By this time, I'd taught poetry for eleven years and read wonderful poems by wonderful students, but never before had I sensed that the poem I was reading revealed a person waking up to his calling.

In the late '80s, most everyone sharing poetry in schools, community centers, drug rehab programs, or prisons talked about "voice." The purpose of our work, the shared rhetoric went, was to encourage others to *find their own voice*. Not a bad mission statement, but it seemed to me everyone already had his or her own voice, and it wasn't so much a matter of finding as of recognizing what was already there. "No Beauty in Cell Bars" struck me as such a recognition. I heard Spoon claim in the poem what had always been his, though even he himself hadn't known.

Writing is often an act of hurling words against the void. Spoon's words didn't feel hurled, but seemed instead to arise from a comfort with silence. Not the silence dictatorships demand of their citizens, the kind poet Stanislaw Baranczak wrote about, ironically, in relation to life in Communist Poland: "If you have to scream, *please* do it quietly." Spoon's silence was closer to the silence Czeslaw Milosz called upon in his poem, "Dedication." Writing in 1945 Warsaw, and dedicating his words to "You whom I could not save," Milosz tells the dead that he has no "wizardry of words." Instead, he writes, "I speak to you with silence like a cloud or a tree."

Beneath Milosz's silence is loss and destruction. The tone of Spoon's silence was longing, for nature and a natural life. In prison, where there's so much sharp sound—those keys, bars, guns being racked— Spoon wrote that he longed for "the silence of a raindrop/Falling gently to earth." Spoon's comfort with silence gave his words the weight of poetry. I assumed this quality was what soon led others at the prison, the men in blue as well as guards and staff, to refer to Spoon as "the poet."

Once Spoon heard his own voice and saw that he could shape it in ways that affected others, he seemed to become as curious about speech as he had been about silence. From his perch in the spiral staircase in front of the education building, most mornings Spoon noted my arrival at the prison. I'd walk to the Arts-in-Corrections office, put down the books and papers I carried, and soon I'd see Spoon at the door. If the small office was full, Spoon would say hello and then leave. If there was space, though, he'd come in and sit down. Just as during his first months in our class, Spoon didn't say much. If a prison official asked me why he was there, I couldn't deliver a clear answer. I'd say "to talk about poems" and that was true but not the whole truth. I myself didn't need to know the answer. Spoon was there, and, as when he walled himself in with chairs in our class, I figured presence was enough of the point for now.

Sometimes Spoon would pick up a book from the stack I'd brought in. "Neruda," I'd say. "You know Neruda. Elmo's favorite poet. He's the one who wrote 'To the Foot from Its Child.' Remember that poem? *The child's foot is not yet aware it's a foot,/and would like to be a butterfly or an apple.*"

"The one where he says the foot is *condemned to live in a shoe*."

"Right."

"And something about a blind man."

"Yes. Here, look," I found the poem in the book and read the line: *Feeling out life like a blind man*.

We were both quiet for a while, *condemned* and *blind man* filling the space of this prison office.

"Where's the dude from."

"Chile. He was from Chile."

"Dead?"

I nodded.

"Chile's in South America?"

"Yes."

"Tell me more," Spoon said and so I did.

"Got any poems by those kids you've been teaching?"

"Yeah," I thumbed through the papers I'd brought and handed two sheets to Spoon.

"No names on these poems."

I shrugged. "The kids are fifth graders. I don't have their parents' permission to show the poems to people in prison."

We paused, listening to what we weren't saying.

"Here, read this one out loud," Spoon requested, passing the pages back to me.

I looked down to see which poem Spoon had chosen, "Okay," I said and then began reading:

My name is like
a hawk flying high
above the clouds.
My name is like the beauty of
a ripe red
strawberry. During
school my name is
fierce at my teacher.
At night my name sleeps peacefully in
the dark of the black.

"'During school my name is fierce at my teacher'," Spoon quoted. "How old is fifth grade?"

"Nine, ten. He's probably ten years old."

While no longer silent, Spoon still seemed less interested in talking himself than in listening to me. He usually mentioned something he'd read or seen on TV, asked me a question about a line in a poem, referred to an item in the news, wondered about beauty or longing or fear, and then sat back and let me hold forth. *Motor mouth* was Spoon's description of my speaking style.

A day or two later, Spoon would be back with a poem he'd written, one inspired by the previous visit. He'd drop the poem off and then disappear. Sometimes I didn't even see him. I'd type the poem twice. Once just as he wrote it and then a second time with suggestions for line break or noting where an image seemed dull. Often Spoon's poem would make me think of a poem by some other poet, or a drawing, novel, or magazine article, and I'd bring in the material to give Spoon when he showed up again.

"Got my poem?" he'd ask at the start of the next visit, and we'd talk about what he had written, my ideas for edits, the poem or drawing I'd brought in and the artist who made it. We'd talk about whatever these topics led to: end-stopped versus enjambed lines, how repetition works in free verse, how an image becomes a cliché.

In most situations in my life, I was the one asking questions and listening to others' feelings and thoughts. I appreciated having someone curious about me, especially since Spoon's questions were ones I could respond to here at San Quentin, where so many inquiries—Where do you live? What does your boyfriend do? Will you show me a picture of your daughter?—were forbidden by the prison rule banning, what was called in the director's rules, "over-familiarity." Best of all, Spoon's questions were ones I often mused upon myself. Our morning exchanges echoed my own writing process of opening my curiosity wide, homing in on a sensation or image, and then putting pen to paper.

"How many poems you got memorized?" Spoon asked.

"I don't know. About an hour's worth."

Spoon smiled. "You measure that way?"

"Well, when I do readings, I'm told to go for twenty minutes or thirty. They give me a time."

"What if you forget?"

"Forget the poem I'm reciting? I have a typed copy in case, but since I don't usually need it, I'm free to look at faces in the audience ..."

"And move your hands around like you do," Spoon imitated my large gestures.

"Yes."

"You feel more free?"

"Exactly. The poem's right there inside me."

We were quiet for a while. Spoon thinking, me gathering poems to photocopy for class that evening.

"Guess," Spoon said, "that's what they mean when they say someone has a poem by heart."

I looked up from my work, stared into some mid-distance above Spoon's head, and then nodded. "Yes. That's just what it feels like. *By heart.*"

6

Diving

BY THE TIME of my talks with Judith, I'd already done some deep diving into myself. I'd spent time with books and subjects I never even dreamed I would study, subjects and books I never knew I could grasp.

This diving started when I first arrived in prison. I told prison staff who interviewed me that I just wanted to do my time, go to school, and be left alone. But I said, if I had to, I would defend myself. I enrolled in the high school and college programs. I took any class the education department had to offer. I even took a class in oceanography. Coming from the desert, such a class seemed absurd to me at the time. But I did have a fascination with creatures of the sea. Also, I had started to appreciate geography and knew I could compare the two in some sense.

Books helped me embrace, and also get away from, the reality of being in prison. How did my life come to this? How did I, someone from the desert, come to prison, a structure I had never seen in person before?

I was angry and disliked authority. Often when an officer barked an order, or just said something to me—even hello!— I would ignore him because both prisoners and officers tested each other, trying to get the other to erupt. Yes, I would obey the rule and follow the order if reasonable. But if an officer persisted in conversing, I would compare their job of turning keys and pushing buttons to one any trained monkey could do.

At the same time, I wanted to make amends for the wrong that had landed me in prison. For any wrongs I had ever done. Not for my sake, but for my mom's sake. I had never seen my mom's face as swollen with fear and concern as when she sat across from me at the brown rusty table at the county jail. At that visit—the one when my father told me "Boy, you better pray"—two cops had stood behind me, waiting to take me back through the heavy grey door with its manila-envelope-sized barred window with a sliding metal lid. I had never seen my mom and dad sit so close together.

Something was taken away from, or killed, in my mom that day. And, at the same time, something awakened and became alive inside me. Why did lives have to be taken and lost for me to wake up, begin my journey, and find meaning in life? I had never set out to kill anyone. I knew that. The universe knew that. If there was a higher power, god or goddess, he or she knew that.

I had finally become conscious of being alive. I believed I could learn something. I believed I had a purpose in life, although I did not know what that purpose would be. I did not know where I was going, but I knew I was going somewhere. This knowledge was fueled by an energy deep inside me, one I had not known I had. I wanted to tell my mom I could now see and feel all the wisdom she had tried to impart to me over the years. I understood now why she had told me not to carry the knife that held my fate. My mom and I knew that her son—her boy, her little Stanley—had been taken away that day in the courthouse as surely as if he had been hung from an old oak tree.

Some innocence died inside me and a sense of guilt and responsibility awakened, forged by a wheel, a circle, of violence, ignorance, and sadness. I wanted to make my mom proud of my worthless life. I wanted her to know that her unconditional faith and belief in me had not been in vain. I wanted to show her, before death took her, that I walked in realness.

Realness is a natural state, unaffected by time or place, an organic truth that comes out uncensored like an unaltered river over a waterfall. A place children have gone to before their truth is altered by environment and society. It is the sweet smell of lilacs without seeing them and the taste of a crisp ripe green apple when there are none around. Realness was that state of letting go when I wrote the poem, "No Beauty in Cell Bars," and I had no idea where the text came from.

Silence, books, and letters showed me my path and kept me growing. I knew to survive I could not fly away. My spiritual diving continued. Why did I have to kill someone? Is there really freedom of choice? I nearly went mad trying to fix what I had broken. How do you bring a life back? How could I make peace? Who could I ask forgiveness from and for some way to honor the loss of life?

I was adrift before prison, and I had to come to prison to find and be who and what I am supposed to be. Signs of my purpose in life started to appear. I began to understand that there is more than one kind of prison. One prison had kept me nowhere but Barstow, and another prison had kept me ignorant of the fact that I could learn and grow. The walls of those prisons had kept me trapped between the discouraging words and paddlings of teachers and principals. Their concrete and bars made me blind and lifeless, as though on a path in a dark forest I did not know I walked on. Bound in those mental and spiritual prisons kept me dreamless, goalless, thoughtless, and hopeless.

Trying to grasp a life without parole sentence was like trying to hold a forest fire in my hands, or an ocean in a tin cup. I knew I had to lose the usual sense of time. Indeed, a day, a month, a year, ten years or one hundred years had to become a moment, a breath in the present. To keep going and growing, I had to let go of time.

I had gone to church every Sunday morning and night for my first twelve years in the free world. I had heard the preachers speak from the Bible. But none of those words spoke to me. Someone told me you must have an open wound on your soul to hear the words. You must be in tremendous pain, like having your heart in a vise, steadily turning—pain you can almost see. Your life must be in the toilet, a turd floating listlessly on its way to the sewer where the waters are cleaned and purified for drinking. It's said that the same waters have been on this earth swaying back and forth, here and there, for billions of years.

I read Genesis and thought the story was a splendid creation. I felt wonder reading how Mother Earth was formed in six days. The Garden of Eden was divine until I read about Adam, Eve, and deception; Cain, Abel and death. I pondered the apple, sin, and nakedness. Creation and the garden were just cream on a rotten pie. I read the Bible from cover to cover. All the violence, some of it sanctioned by God, confused me. All the murders, tribalism, slavery, incest, robbery, mutilation, rape, death, and abuse saddened me. What was good about the book? Why were women responsible for man's fall and for bringing consciousness, death, sex, and sin into the world? Why were people and animals sacrificed? Why did a white dude, who considered himself an expert Bible reader, tell me that black people are cursed to be slaves because Noah's son, Ham, saw Noah naked and therefore hexed all black people into slavery? It seemed to me that all beings—man or woman, white or black—were human.

The stories of the Bible made their god appear like a man and good and evil a part of being human. I read how one must serve and worship only one god, which pre-supposed many gods. I read how there was a devil with many names and states of being, a devil who was given domain over human beings on earth. Satan used to be the top angel in heaven, but when he did not bow to man or god, he got kicked out of heaven, along with a bunch of his followers. Together they ran amuck and raised havoc on this tiny planet in an endless universe. Satan's ultimate goal was to stop human beings from making it to heaven. The devil was lonely and wanted more people to hang out with him eternally in hell. After I read the Ten Commandments, I figured an empty Heaven and no vacancies in Hell.

All of my life I had heard the Bible was a good book, so I thought I must have misunderstood the reading of the Old Testament. I read it again. The same pain and confusion hit me. Why was this book so violent? I moved on to the New Testament and the adventures of Jesus, the Son of God. I liked what he did for the poor, lame, blind, and hungry. I liked some of the wisdom of his words as told by twelve of his companions. Jesus saw no man or woman as better than any other. He did not trip on skin color. The New Testament didn't make everything ugly and evil as the Old Testament did. Jesus spoke of how everyone lived in glass houses, so who could cast stones without busting down their own house? He spoke of love, peace, forgiveness, and the faith of a mustard seed. The story was lovely until Jesus, like Martin Luther King and Joan of Arc, was killed for being loving.

How could Jesus have been murdered in order to wipe away the sins or wrongs of the entire human race? Even for people who did not exist in Jesus' time? If we were all born into sin, had I sinned by being born? Do we choose our own birth and parents? Do we choose our own gods?

I wanted to accept and believe what I read in the Bible because of my mom. I prayed every night for years. When my mom died, it seemed to me that God had punished her for being human. She lived for his glory. My mom had suffered a couple of strokes and could not speak or tend to herself anymore. She had been bedridden for years, lying there, festering, before death kindly and mercifully took her. My mom—who I let down by coming to prison. My mom—who was never loved by my father. My mom—who was never loved by God. There is no way I could believe in such an unfeeling god. No good or evil book could justify doing my mom like that!

I kept my distance from the Bible for a long time and expanded my studies in other areas. I knew there must be some other books full of loving beings, gods or not. I could not accept god being a man when it is obvious men and women come from women. Where were the goddesses? I discovered many goddesses, as well as other beings, nymphs, and fairies, in other religions, philosophies, and mythologies from across Mother Earth: Ancient Egypt, Africa, India, Greece, Asia, and elsewhere. The stories were often not as harsh as the ones I had read in the Bible. The goddesses and other beings sprung from Mother Earth and from universal states such as love, peace, death, life, and romance. These beings gave healing and enlightenment and were not opposed to Mother Earth, but a part of her flow. I could picture beings of all kinds helping some lost child or old person find their way. I could see nymphs and goddesses falling in love with human beings.

One story stood out about a king emperor who created life on earth. He sat in his castle bragging about being the greatest emperor ever. Some entity came down from the heavens and pointed to an endless line of ants crossing the marble floor and said, "See the line of ants beneath your feet. Each one was once the king emperor, the greatest ever."

The stories were packed with wisdom. What mattered to me was the realness imparted by those books and stories. I appreciated how they made me think, feel, and come to know a truth. The more I read, the better reader and thinker I became. I understood that reading enabled me to comprehend subjects and theories that had evaded me in the past. One book often led to other books. Silence helped me concentrate and to see and feel what I was reading. Awe kept my mind, heart, and soul open. My diving led me to believe that I could figure out how to mend the hole in the quilt of humanity that I had made.

Religion led me to mythology and other philosophies. I made an effort to look up and study every unknown word, as a biologist does in a field of unknown plants and flowers. I toyed with new words and used them in my letters. I did the writing and reading exercises at the end of some of the Norton anthologies.

I read that Mark Twain had said, "Never let schooling interfere with your education." So I took college classes, not to graduate, but to stimulate my mind and spirit and to gain more access to books. San Quentin's education, Arts-in-Corrections, and self-help programs seemed endless in those days, a well filled with resources I could use in my quest for self-restoration.

I did not care for the formality of college; I just wanted to expand my ken. I equated philosophy with life and all my studies with wonder, awe, and the need to know and grow. The philosophies inspired me to grasp things in my own way. I read Socrates, Plato, Emerson, Spinoza, and Aristotle. I thought about Liebnitz's view that we live in the best of all possible worlds and Descartes's assertion: I think therefore I am. I cogitated Nietzsche's declaration that God is dead. I thought about Socrates's views that no man consciously does something he thinks will hurt himself and that an unexamined life is not worth living. I considered human beings not as a means to an end, but as ends in themselves. I liked the wisdom of not believing in any country that prospers at the expense of another country.

I studied all the "isms" and "ologies" I could find from Eastern and Western thought. Although Jung, Freud, and Adler fascinated me, I did not like how psychology—which is just a branch of philosophy—chose to break the human being into parts. I believed man to be one with all other creatures and beings, one with Mother Earth, Sun, and Sky. There is no measuring stick that can gauge the depths of the heart, mind, spirit, and soul which are one, and, like the sky, go on forever. You cannot put the universe on a scale and weigh her. No man or woman can look inside the soul, heart, or mind of another like a crystal ball and tell how or what that person will do. I realized that only I could reveal my soul and explore and discover my own truth—my essence, my dark and light beauty, the dark clouds I saw in the sky, or the sweet sunshine I created. When a professor or teacher gave a lecture or an assignment, I checked out my own books on the subject. If what they said did not ring true to my soul, I let the lecture or lesson go. If I was not ready for that particular knowledge, I knew somewhere down the road I would encounter the material again.

I took classes to get a basic foundation in language and reading, to get a structure I could use to learn and soak in things on my own. I dived into a subject until it weighed heavy in me. Books I needed to read began to fall onto my path like ripe red apples from an ancient apple tree. An old prisoner gave me a text full of short verses of wisdom, wise sayings from around the globe. The volume became my bible. I loved and studied that book every day for years. The book inspired my heart and spirit with its insistence on the importance of silence. The knowledge let me know it was okay, and even enlightening, to be silent. I understood that one could hear the whispers of the gods or goddesses. I did not know such wisdom—such depth and magic—existed, created by words. I was in awe, like being back in the desert looking up at a star-filled sky and fat moon where I could fly.

I fell in love with silence and felt she had to be a goddess. I began to experiment, going for days or weeks in silence during lockdowns when we were in our cells twenty-four hours a day. I often looked forward to long lockdowns just for the silence.

I wanted to be silent in this world full of noise, bars, guns, knives, madness, and pain. I wanted to speak only when I could improve on silence. I was amazed by how silence allowed all of my senses to pick up and intensify. I connected to a flow on an invisible level, a level of truth, love, wisdom, and peace. I tasted freedom for the first time in my life and was able to live in the moment. I began to see no boundaries. Talking became irrelevant and, at times, did not affect me anymore. My observation and listening skills became pure in the sense of being clean as a fresh born baby's. Each day I introduced myself to another part of myself.

I thought I had found myself and that I could redeem myself to society. I believed if I grew and bettered myself, I would again taste a sweet summer's breeze. After a decade in prison, I knew I could now do something positive in life. I had read about second chances in Dante's *Inferno, Purgatory,* and *Paradise*; I hoped a second chance would come along for me. I knew I could rise out of hell above ground to live in the outside world again. I could endure any punishment toward redemption: the years and years of ostracism; the lack of hugs, touches, and kisses; the death of family and old River Bottom friends; the riots, shootings, and lockdowns. I hoped to have a chance no longer to be one raindrop on its own having no stream, lake, or river to flow into.

I started to believe in redemption. I probably took all the self-help programs San Quentin offered. I read books on tape for the blind; I took up typing and data processing. During long race wars and lockdowns, I stayed on task. The silence experiments opened me up to the universe—to Mother Earth and what she had to teach me.

I never had the belief in myself that I could be a student, but now I had become a student in life. I longed to one day be accepted as part of the society I had never felt accepted by. From *A Course in Miracles* and Transcendental Meditation, I learned that I die every moment to my old self and am renewed like old skin cells. I found it best to live in the moment and take from the past what enriches the present.

I knew some people would never accept or believe in me and that was okay. I let go of seeking acceptance or approval from anyone. I just wanted to soak in all the knowledge and wisdom I could. I decided to be me despite what guards, prisoners, teachers, or society thought; despite the violence, hopelessness, and stress; despite the longing for nature, a woman, a star-filled desert sky, complete silence, and a peaceful walk on the river bottom. I decided to be me, the best silent being I could be. I discovered that there were entire kingdoms and worlds inside myself. I decided to be me and get to know myself from a silent love and forgiving spirit. I decided to be me despite having one foot in darkness and one foot in light.

I was beginning to understand language—grammar, punctuation, syntax, and parts of speech—but I often second guessed myself because my past encounters with language in school had been negative and so I did not believe I could ever grasp these skills. Nevertheless, I could see the beauty, grace, and power in words; thoughts and feelings rolled around inside me like waves carrying sands and seeds to form new islands.

I was a happy loner and kept what I learned to myself. I lacked the confidence and was too shy to share what I knew with people. Books were my friends, my love, my sadness, my joy, and my freedom. I kept inside even the wonder of the poetry I heard in Judith's class. I never wanted to give up silence. Silence, and also her sister, wisdom, had taught me so much, freeing up eagles, lions, and doves inside my heart. For ten years they had been my guides; nothing could make me venture outside them.

I did not consciously pick Judith for my first two-person diving sessions. This naturally came about after our individual consultation. Judith allowed me the freedom to be my weird, cool self in her class, and that opened the mountain passes to our shared diving conversations. In these, I discovered the importance of questions. I found it was best to do this diving with someone whose feel and flow I trusted instinctively, for both people must speak and listen with their hearts, minds, and souls.

Those diving sessions Judith and I had in the Arts-in-Corrections office often led me to write poems. This process allowed me to bring form to desert stories of jackrabbits and greyhounds, and life to dreams of my mom who had passed on. The diving allowed me to bring to light the pain of seeing my dad going out on my mom, abusing her mentally and physically. The diving also allowed me to forgive my dad before he died.

The diving sessions allowed me to create romance and beauty out of longing for a hug and a kiss. Diving gave me the depth inside to feel and know it's okay just to have deep conversations with a woman. Those diving talks allowed me to feel, link, and see the family that I was born into and my human family in everlasting ways I had never experienced in the free world.

One evening I watched "The Power of Myth," a series of conversations on TV between Bill Moyers and Joseph Campbell. I was blown away out of the cell and taken to uncharted lands, tribes, and kingdoms inside myself and across the globe. Campbell, a philosopher and myth-gatherer, dived into cultures, religions, myths, philosophies of darkness and light, magic and rituals, and blended them all together as my own diving adventures had done. I felt it was okay, that I could perhaps cut a route through my stories and history in my own way, and that I had a path, my own myth and bliss to follow.

I started to put myths to the desert creatures I had grown up around. I put myths or legends to the birds I watched in the plaza. I figured humans, as well as animals, had individual and collective consciousness that led to their own myths.

Judith gave me *The Hero's Journey* by Joseph Campbell, and I went on to read every book of his that I could find. The books enhanced the diving sessions with Judith in the naturally trusting space we created despite the walls, limits, and paradoxes our different cultures and lives brought into focus. Any topic or inspiration that weighed heavy on my heart and soul often came up out of nowhere in our conversations. It was as though we were creating poems as we talked. I found that perhaps some of the things I had to say were important to someone and that the universal is truly personal.

7

Artistic Imperialism

ARE YOU SCARED? most people asked when they learned I taught at San Quentin. No, not really. There wasn't much cause to be scared. First of all, the prison was full of guards, and besides, prisoners didn't often jeopardize the classes or visits they valued. The main reason I wasn't frightened, though, wasn't due to these logical facts but was because Coties, Elmo, Spoon, and the others made me feel welcome, not scared.

Which doesn't mean that I wasn't sometimes uncomfortable as a woman in this intensely male—and sexually charged—environment. Nor does it mean I didn't fret. I worried whether I—middle class, college educated, a born-and-bred good girl—was the teacher my students needed. I was nervous about this, but soon learned I didn't need to be. For the men made it clear that what they wanted from me was whatever I had to offer. *Real* was their highest standard. As long as I—or a guest artist—was honest, sincere, and not driven by ulterior motives, my students were interested in what we had to share.

Even so, I thought a great deal about the implications of the notion of teacher as expert. Every day at the prison, and in the public school classrooms where I also worked, my students—both children and convicts—made apparent that they had their own definitions of poetry. Children often loved best playfulness of language; the men at San Quentin responded enthusiastically to poems they deemed raw or cold, honest poems that were direct and true.

I'd been hired to impart information about image, sound, voice, line, and form, and to bring in material that would invite students to write. Such sharing seemed like a good thing. Still, I was aware that mine was a small swath of poetry knowledge: How could I offer the little I knew without imposing it as god-given truth?

Curious about such questions, I began work on an article in which I wondered if artistic imperialism is inevitable when sharing poetry with people whose backgrounds are different from one's own. Edify, civilize, inculcate, and indoctrinate are among the synonyms *Roget's* lists for "teach." *Civilize* and *indoctrinate* are words with strong histories, especially when the one in front of the classroom is a white woman and her students are mostly black men.

This was 1986, before the onslaught of movies about white middle class women who, in the course of one semester, save an entire classroom of young people labeled "underprivileged," "at-risk," "underserved," or—the most coded descriptor of all—"diverse." Even in the '70s and '80s, though, the storyline of white-teacher-savior was familiar. When I told people the work that I did, a few would get misty-eyed and call me a hero. *Gag me with a spoon*, as we over-privileged, over-served, also-labeled Valley Girls put it.

In the nearly dozen years I'd been teaching, it had never seemed my job to save or civilize anyone. I began what would become my life's work as Sara's mother and, at the start, I thought of myself as a volunteer, a lover of poems, and as someone who had fun sharing imagination with kids. In those days, I didn't even think of myself as a teacher, exactly, for I came to the work so obliquely.

In that time and place—mid-1970s coastal Mendocino County—one could rent a two-bedroom cabin on twenty acres for $75/month or less. We could get clothes at Pay 'N' Take, grow much of our own food and purchase the rest through the co-op, have our teeth cleaned for free at the dental clinic, and barter firewood for a new car engine (or a new car engine for firewood). And all of this while living in what my Aunt Nora called, when my extended family visited, "God's country": redwood, chinquapin, Doug fir, madrone, tan oak, and pine; the Pacific Ocean at our left as we drove north; boletus and chanterelles after the first rain in the fall; the Garcia and Gualala rivers to swim in all summer. The unemployment rate was high in Mendocino County at this time, and it's true, what jobs there were paid very little. Still, most of us didn't need much to get by.

The lack of intense economic pressure allowed one work thing to lead to another. I volunteered in Sara's classes until I was hired to teach a summer school poetry workshop. That workshop led to being asked to join California Poets in the Schools, which encouraged me to talk to the principal about more steady work. For a long while, I was it: the poetry lady in Point Arena and Manchester schools.

I came slowly to calling myself "teacher," though I loved the work and was grateful to so many of my own teachers. In fourth grade, Miss Duque recognized my profound shyness, and her classroom somehow provided both safety and moments to shine. In eighth grade, Mrs. Beckman showed me that I was more able to do math than I feared. Mr. Hatch structured our ninth grade study of history as though we were college students and his complex approach let me know how I best learn. Mr. Cozens modeled for many of us in high school just how interesting talking about ideas could be. Would I have discovered myself as a writer without Miss Grimshaw? Would I feel so at home in libraries without Miss Adams?

I wish I had a mind that retained all the facts that these good teachers taught me, but I don't. What I remember are the doors each opened, the glimpses into a part of the world and a part of myself that I hadn't noticed before. Some of these men and women paid attention to me, Judy T.—Miss Duque certainly did, Mrs. Beckman, Miss Adams. But most were simply good teachers, able to encourage curiosity and creative thinking in even a shy student seated at the back of the room.

I began that article on artistic imperialism by quoting my ninety-year old great-aunt. "Well, dearie," Aunt Irene had written from Colorado, "I'm sure I'm just too dumb to understand, but how does someone *teach* poetry?" I responded by telling Aunt Irene that this was a question I asked myself all the time, especially when I was in front of a group of people who thought of me as the teacher.

Aunt Irene's question raised concerns about cultural definitions of poetic aesthetics. As I say, she was ninety, and the poems she'd read and written as a teenager were rhymed and metered. She wanted to read my poems—all of them free verse—but "honestly, Judy, I can't make heads or tails of them." I think, though, that Aunt Irene was mostly amazed that a process of creation as personal as writing a poem could be taught. I was concerned about both aspects of her question.

In the Santa Rosa Junior College Extension classes I'd taught in Point Arena, many students had grown up on the coast while others were back-to-the-land hippies. Part of the fun we all had consisted of listening to each other. Wherever we'd each come from, here we were, together in this class-room. Here was Sundance with his Ph.D. and bare feet and here was Dorothy with her home-grown conservative values and her sharp wit.

Most of the kids in both Point Arena and Manchester schools were the white Christian children of fishermen, carpenters, or loggers, but others had Pomo, black, Jewish, artist, school teacher, or pot-growing parents. Whoever their parents—water witcher or Natural Foods Store clerk, school bus driver or real estate agent—everyone in the classroom lived in the same community (one that extended twenty miles or so along the coast and four or five miles inland). Our shared world included mushrooms in fall, whales swimming south soon after, baby lambs on the hillside in January, the parade down Main Street on the Fourth of July. We all were familiar with scars in the forest caused by logging and with dead deer on the highway; we all bundled up against the fog, wind, and rain. Gary Snyder's poem, "Hay for the Horses," took place in the eastern part of California "far down from San Joaquin," and not on the coast, but nearly every child I shared the poem with could visu-alize its "winch and ropes and hooks" and the "splintery redwood rafters."

As the years in which I called myself teacher added up, I recognized that a primary task of the job was to develop a constant interplay between the group (with its shared information and values) and the individual (each per-son with her own interests and vision). It was not balance required, exactly, and not compromise. Necessary, instead, was the ability to move quickly from one scale—a whole class discussion of Tu Fu's "Clear Evening After Rain," let's say—to another: bending down by the desk of the third grader writing about a summer afternoon at the ballgame with his grandfather.

In the whole group discussion my job was to ask, "What does Tu Fu say those raindrops are doing to the rocks? Right, 'spatter.' Is spatter like this"—my hands beat the table—"or like this?" My fingers tap lightly and the children call out a unanimous answer. I beat the table again and ask "what are some good words for this sound?" The children brainstorm: pound, hit, smash, pummel. "Those are great verbs," I affirm. "In Point Arena we know rain, right?" The kids groan and nod.

With the individual third grader, my questions arise not from a poem we'd all read together, but from the specific images he saw in his own mind:

Was the sun hot in the park? How did it feel on your head? You write that your grandpa's voice was loud. A drum beat kind of loud? A thunderstorm kind of loud? Oh, a chainsaw kind of loud. Great, I can hear that sound in my head. Here you say your grandpa bought popcorn. Was the popcorn dry or buttery? Oily, huh? Oily as what? The oil your grandpa uses in his shop? Wow, get those words down!

By 1986, as I wrote about artistic imperialism, I was moderately skilled at this teacher's dance of nurturing both the whole class and each individual student, though I'd never studied poetry in any formal way and never studied pedagogy at all. Essentially, I taught myself to teach by paying attention. When I read Ogden Nash's "Adventures of Isabel" to first graders, I looked out into the sea of wide-eyed, open-mouth awe and didn't need the children to fill out an evaluation form. Without being prompted, the children joined in with each repetition of the poem's central couplet: "Isabel, Isabel, didn't worry,/Isabel didn't scream or scurry."

Second graders closed their eyes when I read Victor Valle's "Comida." I could almost see them visualizing "One eats/the moon in a tortilla…" When I asked third graders what they noticed in Lilian Moore's "Winter Dark," their response was the "comma of a moon" and each street light's "period/ to the end of day." These children were studying punctuation and they appreciated having their school studies referred to in the poems I shared. Their teachers appreciated this, too, and I learned to scan each classroom I walked into and to consciously register words written on the chalkboard, charts on the walls, library books on the shelves, and homework assignments lying around on mimeographed sheets.

I saw with my own eyes what worked and what didn't. My first years of teaching were well before today's emphasis on "evidence-based research." I understand why programs have to formally prove their value, but as a teacher, what has always been most relevant is on-the-ground noticing. Are the children excited, curious, and involved? Does the model poem inspire writing? Does the boy who wrote poem after poem about ice cream and candy discover a new subject or express his obsession with some new flourish? Is the girl who only wants to write funny poems about stinky socks sometimes willing to experiment with other subjects? Do the children fade when I talk at length about Emily Dickinson or are they engaged? Do they laugh at my examples of simile? Do some children run up to me in the hallway to show me poems written at home? Is there a parent or two who tells me his or her child now checks out poetry books from the library? Does a classroom teacher let me know that the boy whose poem inspired the whole class to holler and whoop was the very child they'd almost excluded from working with me because he'd always been so unwilling to write? Does another teacher say, "Susan hasn't said one word to us about why she's so sad, but today's poem is all about her mom's illness." Does the principal ask me to stop by her office to ask if I'll share poems at the next PTA meeting? When the typed and stapled anthology appears at the end of the workshop, are the children excited to see their names in print and to read the poems of their friends? Do parents come to the book release reading? Will the SITE committee fund a workshop next year?

When Sara and I moved from the country back to the Bay Area, the lives of the children I taught through California Poets in the Schools were different from the lives of students in Point Arena. In one Oakland school, the 35 fifth graders I met with came from fourteen different countries. In another, third graders wrote poems about the sound of gunshot. In some schools, most of the kids went to child care both before and after the school day; in others, parents stood in the halls at 3 PM waiting to pick up their children and take them to ballet, gymnastics, or judo.

My friend Gail often said that instead of more testing, special programs, and such, children stuck in a building from seven in the morning until six at night needed "fresh air and exercise." Gail intended her words as a funny over-simplification, but she and I both felt they were also true. So many of the children I came to know in Berkeley and Oakland had little or no chance to explore the physical world around them on their own or with some buddies, to sit under a tree and imagine, to ride their bikes to the store having adventures in their minds as they pedaled, or to find a secret safe place to curl up and read a book of their choosing. Such activities seemed almost like Human Rights of Childhood to me and they had been part of the childhood of nearly everyone I knew whether that person had grown up in Los Angeles like me, the Bronx like Gail, Point Arena like Sara, or Khartoum like my friend Sami.

I was thirty-nine in 1986 and thirty-nine is pretty old, really, when you think of the stages of learning, practicing, and mastering one's profession. My teaching practice arose from my instincts, and I honed my approach through paying attention. By this time, almost a dozen years after I first volunteered with Sara's kindergarten class, I could articulate the values at the base of my work.

Imagination is a human birthright: that's where I started. I believed, also, that imagination, and knowing how to distinguish between imagination and perception, is necessary for critical thinking. No matter how vigorously people with agendas—be these parental, pedagogic, political, peer-related, or commercial—try to impose their way of thinking, a healthy relationship with the pictures in our own minds helps us to think for ourselves.

Another central belief is that our stories—the specific life we've each lived, our obstacles and blessings, the people and places we come from, our individual natures—are valid and worthy of being claimed and declaimed. Little children, loggers, hippies, people in prison—each of our stories has value. Equally important to telling our own story is listening to the stories of others; how else will we recognize the whole we're all part of?

A third core belief: pictures, songs, stories, and dance are a direct expression of being human. We come into the world with the capacity to create and everyone—from an infant shaking a rattle to an elder half-lost in the old days—is, in some important sense, making art.

Although a primary task of my work was sharing the tools of poetry, I saw that poems—in addition to being their own beautiful selves—were also a vehicle for a vaster understanding, one that included the above values. As I put the point in a poem about what my students and I shared in our prison classroom: "Call it poems/call it life/call it we breathe and we're human."

I'd once heard poet Robert Bly suggest that if he were running an MFA poetry program, he'd place students in separate cabins in the woods and leave them there for six months to wander, wonder, and write on their own. I'd taught myself about poetry and writing poems in just such a fashion, so I had a great deal of sympathy for Bly's plan.

Still, my San Quentin students were already sequestered. Some of the men spoke of the ways they'd taken advantage of silence and solitude, but most told me that it was the attempt to connect that brought them to writing. Almost every man mentioned writing letters and being surprised at the power his words had to let loved ones know about his experience, to maintain relationships with children, and to woo women. Most of the men I met at San Quentin told me that they had become writers through relationship—with people they loved, with people they hoped to become close to, as well as with their own memories and desires.

This last intimacy, the closeness between each man and his own inner life, was one apparently new to many at Quentin. From what they told me, most of my students had been actors in their pre-prison lives, operating on the surface and enjoying the pleasure at hand. Locked up, their opportunities for action were greatly reduced.

James—a student who joined our class in its second year—put the matter this way on a tape we made that played on the radio: "Here, in prison, where cyclone fences, concrete walls, and steel bars shut out most forms of physical, emotional, and psychological gratification, the power and importance of the mind is evident. Here, most of what we experience that is pleasant must take place in the mind. The feel of a woman's touch, the fragrance of jasmine on a summer day, the sound of the ocean, the taste of hot pizza and cold beer, watching children play on grass in a tree-filled park—these experiences must now take place within the mind because such things are not allowed in the walls of San Quentin. Some people think this process of experiencing pleasures through mental images is no more than fantasy or a symptom of psychosis. But, for me, the poet as well as the prisoner, what I see and experience in my mind is another realm of reality that sustains me in the midst of the bleak reality of prison. And both are equally real."

I could provide some aspects of my students' need for intimacy and connection. Close to forty guest artists visited our class during the four years I taught at San Quentin; we watched dozens of poetry readings on videotape. I created a poetry library and sent our class anthologies, chapbooks, and broadsides to more than one hundred artists, teachers, students, and interested others on the outside. I brought in specific poems for specific interests—William Blake and Kenneth Patchen for Angel—and also a wide range of poets for the whole class: Charles Reznikoff to Victor Hernandez Cruz, Langston Hughes to Mirabai, Allen Ginsberg to Grace Paley, Czeslaw Milosz to Carolyn Forché.

Supporting the intimacy James described—an intimacy with the pictures in one's own mind—seemed to me inherent to the job of a poetry teacher. I thought of this intimacy neither as the "making up" of fantasy or the "storytelling" of recalled events. Instead I agreed with author Haruki Murakami who I heard, many years later, compare this state to dreaming, describing it as "...a way of watching."

Here's what I mean: I sit in the rocking chair, a book in my lap, my eyes in the direction of the open window. It may seem as though I'm looking at the warm breeze lift the curtain from the glass, and in a way I am. But my gaze is too soft, too unfocused, to note much detail about the fabric's loose folds. What arises instead is the smell of suntan lotion, the sight of the pool in Uncle Iz's backyard, the feel of the hot rubber bathing cap as I pick it up from where it's lain in the sun, the sound of my cousin Beryl diving into the pool. I'm not remembering a particular Sunday, or telling myself that after we swim, we'll eat barbequed hamburgers and hotdogs while listening to Vin Scully narrate the Dodgers game on the radio. No, it's not story I'm lost in, but sensory memory.

Such watching seems one gift of being alive, which is why my Human Rights of Childhood include the right of children to lie under trees or sit on front stoops with nothing to do but stare into space. An artist relies on this watching and must develop his or her facility with sensory memory. At San Quentin, I asked my students to close their eyes and simply let a scene arise from their childhoods. *What smell do you smell? What sound do you hear?* Spoon wrote:

> I see the jackrabbit gracefully attempting to flee from the slender
> greyhound who is right on its tail. He catches the rabbit and
> packs it back and suddenly there's another rabbit and there's rabbits
> everywhere. He catches five or six rabbits. But never catches his
> breath so he has gotten caught along with the rabbits and ceases to
> exist.

On a visit to the Arts-in-Corrections office, Spoon asked, "That's how you write poems, huh? Let your mind go loose and see what comes up?"

"One way," I said, relaxing the muscles that lifted my eyelids, letting the lids drift, courting the very state Spoon was asking about.

Spoon said nothing, knowing his silence would spur me to say more.

"It's almost like swooning," my neck and head illustrated the verb. "And in that state of near faint, pictures arise. Pictures, sounds, smells. And I try to both swoon and follow the picture. Guess part of my mind is wide open, and another is totally focused."

Spoon gave a sound half-way between a grunt and a laugh.

"I know, poets are crazy. But, really, that's what it takes: concentration that's simultaneously wide open and totally focused."

"Paradox."

I shrugged. Paradox was a subject Spoon and I often pondered.

"Heard someone on TV describe meditation the way you're talking about writing poems."

Jim Carlson, being funny with googly eyes, 1990.   FAMILY ALBUM

Jim walked into the office just then, picked up three juggling balls from his desk, and began to toss them. "Want to sign up for the juggling class?" Jim asked Spoon. "Starts next week."

Spoon shook his head no.

I thought Jim might try to convince Spoon, but instead he put the juggling balls down and turned to the work on his desk.

Spoon sat without moving, but I felt him wait for my response.

"Maybe," I said. "But in meditation I let pictures and sounds come and go, while when writing a poem I keep my gaze on them steady until words arise and I write the words down."

I couldn't see Spoon's eyes behind his shades, but he seemed to be practicing what I'd just described.

"I guess I try to encourage that state as a teacher." I told Spoon about the afterschool program where I was then working with first and second graders. I described how I put paper and crayons on the table before the children arrived so they could begin drawing when they entered the room. Some kids talked as they drew. I'd listen, ask questions, and when the time seemed right, suggest that we shape their words into a poem. We'd work from what they had been drawing and talking about—*My baby cousin/has a tooth growing in*—and sometimes these details would develop into a more elaborate whole: *The man goes in the car./He goes fast./And then he goes to his house./And he tells his children,/"Do it! Do your homework!/Or you won't go out to play!*

"So the drawing's like wide open concentration and the kids' pictures are like the focus?" Spoon asked.

"In a way. I suppose so."

The telephone rang, and Spoon and I both glanced at Jim as he picked up the receiver. Then Spoon turned back to me, knowing from experience that my mind was likely to leap somewhere, apparently curious about where that might be.

"Have I ever told you the best words I've ever heard about teaching?"

"Can't know till you tell me."

"Right. Well, this was back in the country. After sharing poems, I wailed that I'd interfered too much with the children. The teacher, Mark Morton, nodded. 'That's always the problem,' he said. 'Are you going to teach, or are you going to let them learn?'"

Spoon's lips hardly moved, though I'd have said he was smiling.

"At the same time," I started to giggle. "I mean, remember what Chris"— a new student in our class, a man who had no problem saying just what he thought—"said in class last week when I was concerned that maybe I was interfering or making too many suggestions?"

Spoon sighed, again letting me know I should just, please, answer my own endless questions.

"Chris said, 'Don't worry, Judith. You *know* none of us is going to do what he doesn't want to.'"

8

The Poet

EARLY MORNING and I cut down on at least one cigarette a day. I felt Grandfather's warmth even though he had not made it over the mountains yet. Looking out the barred window, how green the hills and valleys appeared after late rains. In a world of madness, sudden death, and love, the blue skies still seemed placid and unencumbered. I found that, in silence, my head settled down and thoughts were not all over the place but progressed in a unified manner, still twisting, turning, and creating like a stream, but in one flow.

On the prison yard I kept my mask on, my dark shades, non-smiling, dead-eyed gaze, and silence, but when I was back in the cell writing letters, I opened up and released the realness and feelings inside me. Letters were like blood veins or lifelines: I lived through them and only ate and slept in prison. Some people with life sentences think of prison as their home. For me, prison has never been my home, nor could it ever be. That would be like saying slavery is my job or calling. If I'm incarcerated for a thousand years, this place would still be chains, whips, handcuffs, bars, concrete, and steel. No place to keep any human being forever. It's said that home is where the heart is or where one happens to reside on the planet. My home must be in Barstow, Sweden, France, or Norway, where my family is. No cage, physical, mental, or spiritual can be my home.

Over the years I have written letters to many, many people. Some folks now and then have told me I have a way with words. That must be true because my handwriting is so ugly that if my words were not expressed in an honest way, I never would have received any response.

During my first decade in prison, words became healing, powerful, and redeeming. I articulated things and a side of myself I had never spoken of verbally. For the first time in my life, I expressed my innermost thoughts, dreams, and feelings. Letters were like getting a hug or a kiss, like going to the park or the movies. At the start of my journey, letters were the only way to speak my heart without fear of being thought weak.

I came to prison knowing nothing about constructing letters. I just wrote down how I felt in the moment from the feelings evoked while reading someone's letter to me. I learned that the moment is what matters, because who and what I was once was now gone. Who I would become had no bearing on the present.

When people told me I had a way with words, I did not equate that with being a poet and writer. Books led to books and words led to other words. I just wanted to expand in areas I knew nothing about, and my word trail led me to sign up for those two poetry classes.

Besides Judith's class, there was one taught by a guy who wanted to impose his vision and standard of poetry. For me, he left no room for growth. The male teacher tried to be hard in an environment full of convicts. He ripped apart students' love poems or poems of feelings as if they were rags or toys. He reminded me of the white Mr. Williams and the principal from grade school, so I never spoke in his class, not even to wave or say hi, nor did I turn in any work. Soon I decided only to go to Judith's class.

I did not speak much in Judith's class either, but I was inspired, alive, and as though something was thawing out inside. I looked forward to her class each week. I then added poetry books to my studies. There were some wild states inside me, an entire wilderness full of beasts, plants, suns and moons, dragons and all kinds of things that were looking for a realness way to be funneled into the light and love.

Poetry was still a puzzle and mystery, but deep and enjoyable. I began to realize some of the lines in my wisdom bible had come from poetry. I thought poetry must come from some hidden, magical place, a place heavy with knowledge and wisdom. I thought I could never be intelligent enough to write poetry. I now saw poetry in some of the songs of Stevie

Wonder; the Beatles; the Rolling Stones; Earth, Wind and Fire; in some old blues; and the Motown sounds my older brothers Rob and Early Jr. played. Pre-prison love songs now often replayed in my heart and mind.

My first poems weren't free and I felt a void deep inside the heart that did not beat or pump blood. I knew I had tried to be something I was not. I strived to be the moon glowing when I was the sun shining.

Some spirit, muse, or magic moved me to create my first poem one Christmas Eve. I called myself creating a Christmas poem. I sat on my rusty bunk on Bay Side, in West Block, at San Quentin looking out of the bars at the ocean, so close, yet a million miles away. I thought of Christmases past and of not having had one for over ten years. Somehow I let go of my mind, thoughts, and pre-conceived notions of what should and should not be. Some force, some sweet realness, engulfed me. I let go! I let go of the mystery of what a poem should be and flowed with the spirit that moved me. My pen woke up like a drought-stricken land to a roaring tempest.

My first poem flowed in one stroke: "No Beauty in Cell Bars." I wrote the poem on a Friday night and I would not see Judith until Monday. I waited, and when Monday came, I caught Judith in the hallway of the education building and handed her my poem. I had been in Judith's class, shades on day and night, in silence, for over a year. When she read the poem, all she could say—with tear-filled eyes—was "outrageous." She showed the poem to Jim Carlson—the head of Arts-in-Corrections at San Quentin—who was also amazed and to Lynnelle, the painting and drawing instructor, who was blown away. All of them considered me a poet. Yet I did not.

After I began to write, I gradually realized that all my letters had been poetry, too, that all along I had been writing poems. My life was the melody that flowed like a free verse poem. Still, I did not see myself as a poet.

But from the moment I created "No Beauty in Cell Bars," my writing went into automatic. I could write for the exercise; to relieve tension; to assuage loneliness or a broken heart; to grow; to leave San Quentin's walls and bars behind; to clarify a thought, a dream, a feeling, an emotion. I could write for the pleasure it gave me to reread something by my pen. Thoughts and feelings tapped an unknown source inside me and moved my pen across the paper. I wondered where the poems came from.

People from many walks of life—teachers, professors, stockbrokers, college students, and Course-in-Miracles people—complimented me on my work. Reverend Smith at the prison chapel said, "I never liked poetry, but I like yours." I had never heard such kindness about anything I had done before.

One morning people began calling me a poet and "the" poet. I accepted this in silence and wonder, but still I did not believe myself a poet. I was just writing words with no idea of where they came from, and I was stunned at how they arranged themselves on the pages. My command of grammar and penmanship had always been awfully bad. I still heard the berating voices of the teachers and principal from grade school telling me, as well as showing me with the paddle, that I was too stupid to amount to anything, especially anything of note. I felt too uneducated in the nuances of English to be a poet. I had failed in all of my language composition and grammar classes throughout my schooling in the free world.

So I told myself people were just being polite, kind to a fellow human being, when they appreciated my poems. Besides how could I take credit for these poems, or own them, when I did not know where they came from?

But people's words inspired me and evoked more thoughts, letters, words and poems. I found myself naturally making poems inspired by the world, animals, life, and the people around me. I tapped into a pool of realness I never knew existed. I shared this truth with people just to see them smile, if only in their letters to me. This sent floods of joy to my soul, like music. Still, I did not think of myself as a poet.

And then came a glorious day, one where the sun kisses you the moment your eyes open, one where you know something wonderful is going to happen, although you have no idea what it is. I rolled with the flow like a young eagle, aware for the first time of what his wings were for, dancing in and out of clouds.

As I had done each Monday morning since writing my first poem, I went to meet Judith. I sat in my spot on the twisting metal stairs that wrapped around the education building. These stairs led to the upper floor of the education building where there were four classrooms. The first two classrooms were empty. The back two classrooms, overlooking the lower yard and Mount Tam, were teachers' offices and storage rooms. Right down the middle of the four classrooms was another staircase that led down to the bottom floor and straight on to the garden plaza. The big, green, wood-framed glass doors were always double locked. They were hard to look into, but easy to look out of. I often hid all day on those stairs reading, pondering, and studying. This was the most peaceful and silent place I could find and before I knew about Judith, poetry, or Arts-in-Corrections, I often spent my day on the hidden stairs.

On this glorious day I left my outside perch and went up to the Arts-in-Corrections office. I knew Judith taught poetry to youth in schools. Sometimes she shared prisoner poems with the youngsters and one time a few had responded to me.

I sat down in the chair next to Judith's desk and we exchanged greetings. She seemed unusually giddy, happy like a spring sparrow. She said, "Spoon, guess what?"

I was not much into "Guess what?" games and Judith saw I had no clue, so she continued. "I read some poems by the men in our class at Point Arena Elementary School," she pulled out a bundle of letters and tossed them to me, "and the kids loved your poems and wrote these poems and letters."

I always wore dark shades. I hardly ever smiled, talked, or took these shades off. Even on the most wonderful of days, I kept the wonder of it all inside me. But as I read the kids' poems and letters, my glasses no longer served their purpose. So I took them off. My shades could not mask the awe. I could not contain the magnificence, the pure joy bouncing off the pages into my heart and soul. Before I even asked Judith if I could keep the poems and letters, she said, "I have to ask Jim."

Jim already knew about the kids' writing and had come into the Arts-in-Corrections office without my noticing, for I had not lifted my eyes from the poems and letters. Jim said, "I don't see why not."

"Is it cool for me to answer the kids letters?"

Jim and Judith looked at each other and Jim said, "That could be something real. A letter exchange between students and prisoners."

"Sure!" Judith said. "I talked about that with a couple of the teachers. Everyone was excited. They said you could write to those children whose parents give permission. You could write to the school, so no personal addresses would be given."

"I can take the letters then?"

"I'll check with the public information officer to make sure, but I see no problems," Jim said.

I sprung out of the office like a young man who had just found his calling. I went to my hidden stairs and pondered the poems and letters.

83

Then I ran around showing the kids' work and my own poems to people, even people I did not know or like. My existence on this rock finally had meaning—a beat, a pulse, a path. The whole day was enhanced with such joy. I bounced around smiling inside and out. For the first time, I felt like a poet!

I had already begun to form the letters to the kids. I would tell them about my pitfalls that led me to prison and, hopefully, help them avoid any similar fall. I wanted to tell them that prison is not cool and to tell them about the wildflowers, soft desert sands, and warm summer breezes I missed. I wanted to impart the knowledge that they could make it through school if even an outsider like me had managed to do so. I wanted to let them know how it feels to think you are unloved and alone, and to tell them that they could make it through the uselessness, the emptiness, the loneliness, the growing pains, and the love pains. I knew how it felt to be hit upside he head with extension cords and chopped off water hoses; I knew how it felt to want to be dead.

Since my writing had gone into automatic, I kept my binder of poems with me ready to share my work with people coming in to the prison with the personal expansion groups, church or pagan programs, or as visiting artists, college students, and teachers. I placed the kids' poems and letters in my binder and I kept taking the text out, reading the kids' poems and letters over and over. Each reading sent joy to my soul like reading Kahlil Gibran.

The next day, I was summoned to the office and as soon as the door opened, a frost feeling hit me, a cold cutting wind bit my heart and soul. Something told me the prison powers-that-be could not allow someone to smile inside and outside from behind walls, where the only right one has is to breathe. And often it is made plain that if one becomes too wise and too human, even that one right will be prohibited.

I sensed something was wrong in Judith's and Jim's faces. It seemed like their voices and spirits strained to say something their bodies and hearts did not want to say.

Jim spoke first, "Spoon, I am sorry, you cannot keep any of the kids' poems and letters."

I said nothing.

"You cannot write any of the kids, either."

Still I stood silent.

Judith spoke, "I thought this could work, Spoon. I still think the exchange is a good idea. The administration says they don't want to set any of you prisoners up as heroes."

Heroes! That shit, that bullshit, never even entered my mind.

Jim said, "The public information officer asked, what if a prisoner gets out and goes and does something to one of those kids?"

I thought: What if the oceans stopped being water and became fire? What if the sun stopped shining and all the trees died? What if the moon became the sun? I sat there in prison, serving a life sentence. Nearly everyone in the poetry class was a lifer. Besides, the letters were to me; I would be the one to write back, not a whole block of prisoners. The absurdity of the situation stunned me. I sat in silence for a few moments until I felt my legs and heart again. I looked up, looked at Judith and Jim and then at the floor. I put my shades and frown back on, and without a word I handed them the kids' poems and letters and left. I sought a place to be alone. Then I realized in hell it is always hot; there is no shade.

I sat in my spot on the metal stairs outside the education building. People found out what happened and some said, "At least you got to see those poems and letters." At least you got to see them. Words sometimes do not fill the space, just like a drop of water does not make an ocean or river.

Back in the cell, I sat down in darkness and silence amid a loud world and recalled the day. I lay on my rusty bunk and pondered the pain; how could I make something of it? How could I make the moment true, or breathe hope into the sadness.

It was Friday and I would not see Judith and Jim again until Monday. Judith often spoke about the paradox of my being in prison and human, and her being a poet/educator working in a prison and also human. So when something came up that impeded a human exchange between prisoners and kids—or the public in general—Judith understood and embraced a paradox of how to stay within the bowels of the rules, even the inhuman, nonsensical ones, the rules set in place only to punish and dehumanize.

I had found my niche, my own humanity, through my journey, studies, and poetry. I had uncovered inside myself a way of transforming my anger, sadness, pain, and unrealness into art by embracing the moment. I often took umbrage at rules that were there just to further punish and humiliate prisoners, rules put there to incite and make a person turn more animal-like instead of redeeming himself. I knew how to be a robot and an animal just for the sake of destroying things and hurting people. For self-rehabilitation, or any kind of restorative work, to succeed, there must be constant contact and exchange with the public, people of all ages, colors, and cultures. There must be continuous dialog and programs that put mirrors up to everyone's faces, not just the prisoners.

I finally knew I was a poet and not a "prison poet," a being I do not believe can exist. I knew I had found my path and what I did best in life. I had humbly become a poet. A note from poet Richard Wilbur in which he agreed with my assertion that poetry allowed a huge part of myself to be free; a copy of *I Know Why the Caged Bird Sings* in which Maya Angelou signed "poet on in joy, Spoon Jackson"; compliments from Ms. Ruby Dee; Martin Esslin advising me to keep writing and sending my work out; and Barney Rosset telling me that he was thinking of ways to get my poetry out in the world all would help confirm my destiny. But the most important confirmation had come from the kids—the young people—at Point Arena Elementary School.

Monday came and I was not on my spot outside the education building. I am sure Judith and Jim wondered where I was. I turned up at the office later that day and handed Judith a new poem, "Right Now I Choose Sadness." I handed her the poem and then left.

9

Way Out in the Bay

A s a teenager I longed to be part of Gertrude Stein's Saturday evening salons at 27 Rue de Fleurus or the gathering of painters and poets at the Cedar Tavern in 1950s New York. The Judith in my imagination didn't sit in corners observing, didn't drop food from her cocktail napkin, or trip over her own words. This Judith moved her body like a silky dress hanging on the line in a warm evening breeze, like a dress—as I once read in someone's description of sexy—one could slink around in. Her mind, too, was loose and agile. I imagined this Judith's hair more auburn than mine, her eyes one degree more hazel; she was taller, thinner, a hundred times more graceful. She could wear high heels and not wobble, talk in straightforward sentences rather than spirals of speech; she could, and did, flash a seductive half-smile instead of a sincere mega-watt blaze. She had my name and my interests—books, paintings, art-making—but she was hardly like me.

Instead of attending salons, or their teen-age equivalent, I stayed home and imagined the group of artists I would someday be part of, or the artist lover I'd live with in a tiny cabin by the ocean. He and I would spend our days and nights writing, painting, walking, making love, and talking deep talk. No bills, grocery shopping, or trips to the doctor. Nothing mundane: a life with only the high points. I was more myself in this artist-lover story— shy, intense, needing protection from too much stimulation—than I was in the dress-you-could-slink-around-in fantasy, but I had no idea how to make either dream real.

By chance and good luck, I met Ronnie when I was eighteen and in many ways the life we shared for close to fifteen years was a real-world version of the by-the-sea story I'd visualized. We were both shy, both loners, and though we talked a great deal about artists whose work we loved, a Rue de Fleurus/Cedar Tavern life remained remote fiction.

I spent my twenties in an era—the mid-1960s to mid-1970s—notoriously wild and communal. Drug-enhanced or served straight, creativity was valued and everywhere were poems in political newspapers, posters for rock concerts, theatrical happenings, and songs against the war. The open invitation of those years was extended to those not in the mainstream art world. From Judy Baca's mural group SPARC (Social and Public Art Resource Center) in Los Angeles to the multi-media arts and education focus of Appalshop in Kentucky, from San Francisco's Neighborhood Arts Program to Elders Share the Arts in New York, people and programs spoke up for work that included the vision and voices of entire communities and not only those of individual genius artists.

My coming-of-age had been shaped by such communal effort, especially by the civil rights movement. As a teenager I sang "We Shall Not Be Moved" and "If You Miss Me from the Back of the Bus" with my whole heart, although my body was far from Selma and in no way on the line. A few years later, I did my share of anti-war work and certainly felt the generational pull of the era. But the fundamental, day-to-day, reality in my twenties and early thirties was of being lovingly swaddled in the cocoon Ronnie and I wove together, first in Berkeley and then on the coast. Until the swaddling tightened and all I knew to do was to break out.

In her introduction to *The Western Edge*, a book of Mendocino County poems that came out in the late 1970s, Sharon Doubiago described the collected poets as a "community of individuals." The town of Mendocino, although still a village, was large enough to speak of as a community in this way. The Art Center hosted a reading series and welcomed visiting poets; the local radio station produced a weekly poetry program; small presses published books, magazines, and anthologies. Poets gathered in cafés and bars to talk. Robert Bly gave a reading in Mendocino in those years, as did poet Maxine Kumin.

Moving down-coast, though, sixteen miles south to Elk, another nineteen to Point Arena, and ten miles more to Anchor Bay where Ronnie and I had hand-built our tiny home, the "individual" in Doubiago's equation assumed a different relationship to "community." Towns were smaller on our part of the coast, more cut off. Literally cut off a few times most winters when rain and high tides caused the water to rise over the Garcia River flats, flooding the highway, and putting a halt to traffic for a few hours or days. Not many of us south Mendocino coast poets were Cedar Tavern types. We were more likely to sit at each other's kitchen tables and talk about poems over hot tea.

Her kitchen table is precisely where I met Kate Dougherty. Kate taught poetry at Greenwood School in Elk, her children's school, and I walked into her kitchen because I'd read an article she wrote and thought from her words that she might be a kindred spirit. Kate made us tea and our conversation—about writing, teaching, being mothers, and especially about poems—spread out over the afternoon and into the months and years ahead.

Judith with Kate Doughtery, mid-1990s   FAMILY ALBUM

Kate and I were country neighbors, which means we lived twenty miles apart. We sent each other poems, comments on poems, questions about poems, sent haiku and haiga through the mail. We recommended books, lent books, quoted from books. After I returned from Europe, Kate taught me the basics of letterpress printing in Elk. I'd drive back to Point Arena and tack the broadsides I'd printed to the bulletin board outside the general store.

The two of us wanted so much! We tried to write the best poems we could, of course, but also we pledged ourselves to the entire endeavor of poetry. We didn't know if we'd chosen, or if we'd been chosen, but by the time we met each other our feet were well set on a path that required a commitment to seeing the world and ourselves as we were. Kate and I worked hard to develop an almost flat voice; we refused to lure a reader in with high jinx or drama. We wanted our poems to speak from a point of view distant enough to allow far-sighted vision. At the very same time, we insisted—to each other and on the page—that the core of each poem was hot, never cold, and came from passion, caring, engagement, and love for the world and each of the world's manifestations.

We studied poems, taking them apart to see how they worked. We'd choose a poem, James Wright's "A Blessing" for example, sit at our separate desks at night after our children had gone to bed, and open our copies of *This Branch Will Not Break*. I usually typed the poem we'd chosen so that I could mark the page as I scanned the lines for stressed and unstressed beats, repeated vowel sounds, extended imagery, alliteration, and other tools of the trade.

Kate and I typed up our notes for each other into nearly short essays. Then we'd isolate one detail—that famous enjambed line at the end of Wright's poem perhaps—

Suddenly I realize
That if I stepped out of my body I would break
Into blossom.

—and write poems of our own using that inspiration as model.

I worked on a big, office-model, manual Olympia in those years—so solid that I could type as fast as my fingers were able, which was very fast, without the machine moving from the pad on which it rested. Those keys struck with a heavy plunk into the country night. Many years later, Sara told me that the sound that made her feel safest was that of typewriter keys, the sound she most often fell asleep to as a child.

Next time I was in town, I'd mail off my notes to Kate at the post office. Or I'd leave them on her kitchen table if I was driving north. Unlocked doors and manual typewriters: our lives on the coast in the early 1980s.

I'd await Kate's poem study notes with almost the excitement of waiting for love letters. They *were* love letters, really, full of love for this art we cherished and steeped ourselves in, this art we were then giving our lives to.

At San Quentin, I told Spoon about Kate and about how she and I had been each other's MFA program. "Once, when my heart was broken, Kate sent me Emily Dickinson's 'After great pain, a formal feeling comes…'" I recited the poem for Spoon and told him how memorizing it led to my learning the dozens of poems I had by heart.

"One time," I laughed as I remembered, "I was walking along the highway, memorizing a poem. I saw the school bus pass, and later that evening, Sara complained that she'd had to tell her friends that her mom wasn't crazy, talking to herself, but only saying poems out loud."

I talked with Spoon about the north coast world Kate's and my poems grew from: copious rain most winters, sorrel in spring, the Navarro River north of Kate's, the Garcia and Gualala rivers I swam in on my part of the coast, Mrs. Berry across the street from Kate on Greenwood Road, dances at the Upstairs in Point Arena. And Spoon spoke of the country he'd come from—the heart of the high desert, soft sands by the dry river bottom, B Hill, railroad tracks, Blacks Bridge, and Crooks Street.

"Wild wet winter," I said to Spoon.

"Alliteration," he replied.

"Yes, and also the truth." For, on the ridge above Point Arena, the average annual rainfall tended to be sixty inches, almost all of it in the few months between November and March. *Wild wet winter* wasn't just clever language, but also an invocation of fallen trees blocking dirt roads, the sound of surf in a storm, the memory of 1983's endless downpour when the pier and the boathouse were ripped from the wharf.

I talked with Spoon about the season word in haiku, cherry blossoms or the *uguisu* that mean spring to a Japanese reader. I told him that in Point Arena our season words might be amaryllis, wood smoke, rhododendron, and wind. "Sometimes I feel uncomfortable using these words," I said. "They can seem too easy, just quaint, to a reader for whom they are mostly sounds."

I read Robert Hass's "Spring Drawing, II" out loud to Spoon, emphasizing:

> Suppose before they said *silver* or *moonlight* or *wet grass*, each
> poet had to agree to be responsible for the innocence of all the
> suffering on earth.

"I think of that line just about every time I sit down to write a poem," I said. "Like a prayer."

I told Spoon that in a Point Arena poem *dry grasses*, for example, had harder work to do than merely to paint a tawny watercolor wash of late summer. The phrase had to summon a world of specifics: It's August, the days are still hot, but afternoon light is already red-gold and falling lower to earth. School hasn't started back yet and the children still holler as they swing on the rope under the bay laurel. Now the adults clean their chain saws and drive into forests to cut wood for winter. Kitchen windows are steamy from canning fruit and making jams and sauces. Around the dinner table friends wonder if there's still time for one more hike up the river.

Amaryllis, dry grasses, apples cooking down into sauce. Mendocino coast season words.

"Why don't you invite Kate in as a guest artist?" Spoon asked.

So I did. Our class had published two anthologies by this time and we were about to launch a chapbook series; I envisioned one small booklet of poems by each man. Kate shared dozens of examples of her own printed creations, giving design advice to my students.

I also told Spoon about Myrna Scott, whom people in Point Arena referred to as "The Poet" in the same way that Spoon was called "The Poet" at San Quentin. I'd first heard Myrna read at the Upstairs. There was a lot of mediocre poetry recited that night, as there is at any open mike, but then one frail woman stood in front of the crowd and read in a cigarette-thickened voice:

> the sea reaches out to me
> as a mother to a child.
> there is kinship between blood and brine.

I carried the moon in my womb half a lifetime
and the moon carries the tides.
something strong within my soul
remembers when I was a fish,
and the rhythm of my heart is the rhythm of the sea.

Myrna lived alone in a house just up from Point Arena's Main Street, and I often stopped by when I was in town. Nine times out of ten I found Myrna sitting in the corner of her couch, her tiny figure bent over a green steno pad working on a poem or copying lines from one of the books stacked on the coffee table. An ashtray was placed on the couch's armrest, and a mug of coffee as well. If Myrna had been feeling well enough, she might have walked the couple miles to the sea earlier in the day, or gone into town to pick up a few staples. Sometimes one of us, her friends, did her grocery shopping and occasionally Myrna allowed us to drive her to look out at the ocean.

Mostly Myrna hid. Soon after I met her, she told me, as she'd told others, that the FBI had been following her for years. She said the surveillance had started when she was a young mother. This was the mid-1970s—after the Bay of Pigs, Cointelpro, Watergate—and I had no reason to doubt that the FBI had targeted Myrna. It took awhile to realize that this FBI harassment was a stand-in for all Myrna's fear and for her sense that she would always be thought wrong.

Myrna had been raised on a ranch near Sacramento. Her favorite child-hood memories were of her father taking her in the truck as he made rounds. She was the child chosen because, her father told her, she knew how to keep quiet. As a young woman, she took in the infant of an unmarried friend. She longed for her own baby, too, though when her son was born, her husband disappeared. She worked as a waitress in Mill Valley raising her boys and writ-ing poems. By the time I met her, Myrna's children were grown and gone, and SSI—one gift of the paranoia—paid her few tiny expenses.

A half-dozen women, most of us two or more decades younger than Myrna, felt for her wounded spirit. We also learned from her. For despite physical and mental misery, Myrna consistently worked to keep her heart open. She sat on her couch, coffee and cigarettes at hand, with the sole purpose of waiting for the Muse and any line She might offer. Myrna's bent body was receptive: to wind and rain (the weather she loved), to the sea and big storms, to her young friends and the stories we told from our full active lives, to poems by the children I taught. Myrna was in her sixties but her lined face and hoarse laugh seemed ancient.

I shared with my San Quentin students my favorite of Myrna's poems. These poets were such young men, and I knew they might hear Myrna's submission as weak. Still, I hoped some would notice the freedom her poem finds in acceptance.

BIRTHDAY PARTY

do not bring me rejuvenating
mineral water or teas,
do not bring me creams
ointments, hair dyes
or exercise contraptions.
let me have my flabby belly,
it has known girdles, pregnancies
paralysis, four operations
and endless pain.
let me have the lines in my face
deepening, as a winter night,
some of sadness, some of joy
a miniature of my soul,
half a century
reaching out, accumulating.
let me have my gray hairs
each one marking a sleepless night
a lost poem, a dead dream.
let me have my unsparkling eyes
they have seen most
of the contradictions,
love hate, seas deserts
happiness sorrow, mountains plains
sex celibacy, birth death.
let me have my bent shoulders
and the hidden tears they carry,
they have endured too much
of poverty, persecution

injustice and madness.
let me have my slow walk,
like a small mountain stream
I was once running young.
once is enough.
let me feel life's salt,
old as the sea.

Sometimes those of us who loved her talked with each other about trying to make Myrna see that the FBI was not following her. But it didn't take long to realize that our friend had come up with a perfect metaphor: the FBI for everything in her life that had harassed her. Take away the FBI and, we were all pretty sure, Myrna's ability to function at all—alone there in her house with her cat, cigarettes, coffee, and poems—would crumble completely.

Myrna called one or the other of us when she was especially sad or scared. We'd come over or just talk to her on the telephone in the middle of the night. After I'd moved back to Berkeley, Myrna called to ask about the children I taught and the men at San Quentin. She wanted what I could tell her of their stories and poems. She was encouraged by the words of others who wrote in the face of difficulty: the boy from El Salvador who missed his grandparents at home, the girl whose father had been an architect in Poland but could only find work as a janitor since coming to this country, Elmo who was serving a life sentence although he'd killed no one, Spoon who was growing into the knowledge of himself as a poet.

Most of Myrna's poems were lyrics, but she loved the haiku form and all her work had qualities of the haiku—from the way she understood her place in the world ("let me be so free/that I am chained by a fawn,/shackled by a cloud or a stone"), to her sad-tinged recognition of the solitary essence of being human.

This tone was also Spoon's tone, the tone of silence inside the noisy dungeon of prison. I gave Spoon poems by the masters—Basho, Buson, Issa—and shared my favorite contemporary haiku, one written by Myrna with an Issa-like laugh:

strong north wind
haggling with my hat
over where my hair should be

Spoon ended up in prison and Myrna ended up crazy, but they both had discovered themselves as poets, and that discovery meant—if not everything—an enormous amount to each.

Kate and Myrna were both part of my Mendocino coast poetry salon, a psychic salon I suppose, each one of us writing poems in her own separate cabin. Although I remained too shy even to be part of the poetry scene in the town of Mendocino, I still loved imagining Rue de Fleurus and Cedar Tavern. In fact, the book I had been reading in the days before leaving my marriage was James Mellow's *Charmed Circle: Gertrude Stein and Company.*

Neither *Charmed Circle,* my imagination, nor any over-blown sense of self-regard, had led me to think that by leaving my marriage and heading for Europe I would end up in the company of contemporary Steins, Matisses, and Picassos. Besides, if I was too shy for Mendocino, I was unlikely to sparkle in Paris. No, I hadn't left for the sake of a fantasy, but because of a vow. This troth wasn't the one I'd given to Ronnie, or even to Sara—though my vows to my daughter were forever, unbreakable, and with my whole being. This promise was instead made ages before, in childhood, or maybe even earlier somehow. I may well have come into the world with this intention planted in my tiny heart: to live life deeply, intimately, and open to spirit. Perhaps this is the vow that created such a hypersensitive Princess and the Pea. At any rate, although the safe harbor of marriage had been sweet—I probably would not have survived without its protection—the buffer eventually felt like avoidance.

Poems accompanied me on the journey to Europe, poems I wrote and poems I read. Then I returned to the coast, studied poetics with Kate and memorized poems as I walked through forests, along rivers, on the side of the highway as the school bus passed, and by the sea. And soon poems took me to prison.

I first went inside to visit classes taught by my friend, Larry. I'd spent a lot of time with Larry and his partner, Rojelio, during my last couple years on the coast. Record albums were stacked around all four walls of their living room, the study's bookcases were full, an ink drawing or collage was always in progress on the table. As soon as I walked through the front door of their home, Rojelio grabbed my elbow. "You have to hear this," he'd say, as he put on the turntable X, the Velvet Underground, or Patti Smith.

Rojelio and I developed performances of the work that we loved. He read "Macario" by Juan Rulfo and Octavio Paz's "Head of an Angel" and

"The Blue Bouquet." I recited poems I'd memorized by Milosz, Baranczak, Zbigniew Herbert, Vallejo, and Neruda—Eastern Europeans and South Americans who knew what it was to live under repression.

Just before Sara and I returned to the Bay Area, Rojelio and Larry moved to Bakersfield in Southern California. Larry got a job teaching at the prison in Tehachapi, and he invited Rojelio and me to come in to share the work we'd been performing. The men in Larry's class responded with intense attention. The questions they asked and the memories they shared seemed fueled by a hunger I felt myself: a longing for poems powerful enough to help find a way through hard times. The tone in Larry's classroom was similar to that of my one-to-one poem talks with Kate or Myrna, but this was a group, not a single shy friend across the kitchen table. Together we acknowledged and held both the suffering and beauty present in the room with us.

That day inspired me to look for a similar classroom closer to home; that search took me to San Quentin. And now, here we were—Coties, Elmo, Spoon, the twelve other men in our class, and I. Most of my students faced some kind of life sentence and had done serious thinking about their lives, about life, and about what it is to be human. They brought this thinking to the poems we read and they wrote. Everyone in the room, each of the men and me, too, had suffered and had caused suffering. None of us felt comfortable with the world we'd been given; none of us felt we fit in. We were oddballs together, making the best of what we had. We made room for each other in the space that we shared in a way that I wasn't used to, but had always hoped for.

No one would call our prison class a "charmed circle." There were no Picassos on the wall, no Matisses; the fluorescent lights and wall of Plexiglas made for an ambiance quite different from that of 27 Rue de Fleurus. Our night ended when count cleared, most often somewhere between nine and nine thirty, and did not extend into the wee hours as at Cedar Tavern. But I felt I'd found the group of artists that was mine to belong to, here at San Quentin, in our buried classroom, way out in the Bay.

10

Godot

MY SENSES WERE on full alert as I felt someone watching me. A thin, blond, white man had his eyes on me. But my instincts told me his gaze was foreign, one of curiosity and not of a negative nature. Judith and Jim told me that the skinny guy was Jan Jonson, a trained actor and director from Sweden. He had come to America to do some stage play called *Waiting for Godot*, written by some Nobel Prize winning playwright, writer, and director named Samuel Beckett.

Jan, with Samuel Beckett's support and blessings, had done *Waiting for Godot* at Kumla Prison in Sweden. Jan—again with Beckett's full support—had now come to America, to San Quentin, in early 1987, in the hope of directing the play at the prison.

Jan watched me for a reason. He had read some of my poetry and wanted me to be a part of the production. I had never heard of Samuel Beckett, Jan Jonson, or *Waiting for Godot*. I had never read or seen a play before, never imagined myself acting on a stage.

When Jan approached me about portraying Pozzo, I thought the idea of a human being deprived of freedom being in a play was insane. Especially me, Spoon Jackson, a loner, a lover of silence and silent things, a shy observer of self, life, people, and Mother Earth, a man who had only a few words to say in private now and then.

Jim, Jan, and Judith filled me in on Samuel Beckett and *Godot*. Mr. Beckett was sometimes called the modern-day Shakespeare and his play, *Waiting for Godot*, was world famous and translated into many languages in many countries. Jan told me that Mr. Beckett loved silence in his personal life and used silence in his plays. I had nothing in my life to compare to doing a play—a play, on a stage, before an international audience. Besides, although I was a poet, I had never read aloud one poem in Judith's poetry class. How could I get on stage and portray a character in a two-and-one-half to three-hour performance?

So, out of fear of the unknown, I said no, I will not be in the play.

Jan went back to Sweden and I went back to my silent world full of poetry bursting to be said aloud. Jan told me he would be back later in the year to hold auditions but that I could be Pozzo if I wanted. I had time to ponder things. Judith told me how much Jan liked my poetry. It was splendid that someone from the other side of the planet saw and felt my work, that someone believed in me even though he did not know me and had not heard me speak any poems. But how could he think I could act in a play?

Jim and Judith told me how beneficial being in the play might be. How it could open new worlds and ways to get my poetry out. I thought long on what the play could mean and be in my life. I spoke more with Judith and Denise—Jim's boss at the prison and a big part of the arts program. They both accepted my admonishment that if I did the play and anything went wrong, it would be their fault! I had no idea what could go wrong or right or in-between the two states. But with Jim's, Denise's, and Judith's full backing, I had some foundation, some platform, to grasp and stand on.

During the months Jan was back in Sweden, Judith offered a short class on Samuel Beckett. We watched "Rockaby" with Billie Whitelaw and Laurel and Hardy movies. We met Joseph Miksak who had been in the San Francisco Actors Workshop production of *Godot* in 1957 when the group brought a performance of the play into San Quentin. When Jan returned, I agreed to be Pozzo. Jan began the auditions and after a couple of weeks, the cast was chosen.

Jan began to introduce his world as a Shakespearean trained actor and director. He began to unfold Beckett's world and the world of *Waiting for Godot*. Jan not only knew Beckett, but he was one of the few people

Beckett considered a friend. Jan brought in other old friends of Beckett to speak with us.

Jan shared the film made at Kumla. This film showed how the cast in Sweden had rehearsed and developed the play. He told the story of the cast being scheduled to perform before a live audience in Sweden and how this did not happen. The Kumla cast's opening performance was to be in a theater outside the prison, in the city of Goteberg. The audience became restless waiting for the curtain to rise. Jan brought a stool on the stage and sat silently for a few moments. He shook his head, wiped his face, and smiled. He told the audience that all but one of the actors—the one who played Pozzo—had escaped. Again, a long silence prevailed in the theater.

Jan—an animated storyteller—told the audience how he met Mr. Beckett and how they became friends. He spoke of *Godot*, his Kumla cast, and how he had developed the play at that prison. He spoke of the actors and the countries each was originally from. Jan entertained the audience for nearly two hours. By the end of Jan's speech—performance—the audience thought that the actors' no-show was very Beckettish. They felt as if they had waited for Godot. Even Mr. Beckett smiled when he heard the story, enjoying the irony of no performance.

When Jan approached Samuel Beckett again about doing *Waiting for Godot* in prison—this time in America—Beckett whole-heartedly agreed. Beckett believed that prisoners, particularly lifers, shared a reality with his play that could not be captured or expanded on in other circumstances, a reality of nothingness, smallness, timelessness, emptiness, and the waiting for what does not happen.

The San Quentin cast sat around a long table. Jan handed us scripts that had been autographed by Beckett. There we were: Jan, the actors, and the scripts. I perused the play over and over again in my cell before we sat down for a second time at the long table for a dry reading. Jan told us he'd called Samuel Beckett on the phone for advice. Beckett's voice, presence, and spirit hung around us throughout the development of the play.

For me, the entire play was one long masterpiece, a poem of life in two acts. I watched, listened, and read the text wondering how I could remember all my gestures, lines, cues, and make them live. I liked silences and knew I would have no problem with them. Judith made time to rehearse with me. I discovered that I remembered my own lines, gestures, and cues when I knew everyone's lines, cues, and gestures, too.

The play progressed. We moved from the round table to an empty classroom. Jan had chosen Ralph—a chubby, balding man with a long beard—to play Estragon. Ralph had studied drama and had read *Waiting for Godot* in college. He had seen the play before. He saw himself as an expert on the play and Beckett. He began to make demands disguised as suggestions to Jan about how the play should be directed, acted, and performed. Finding Jan to be, or seeming to be, a bit timid at first, Ralph became more bold. Jan had chosen Mike—a close friend of Ralph's—to play Vladimir, but even Mike became fed up with Ralph's antics and quit the production. Mike wanted to salvage his friendship with Ralph.

Jan again held interviews for Vladimir and the finalist was another poet from Judith's class named Chris Brown, whose poetry Jan had read. Actually Ralph was part of Judith's poetry class also. He was one of the few white prisoners who stayed in Judith's class when most of the group became black.

I had known Chris for over eight years. We had played basketball and had discussed our lives and different philosophies, politics, and religions. We had become friends. Chris was from Oakland, California, and he hooked me up with a sister out of his city. She, however, did not believe most of the things I said to her because she was not used to guys from the desert.

Chris told me once that he never read anyone's poetry in books, because he did not want it to influence his writing. Chris practiced numerology and charted his life by the stars. He often said that the constellations predicted he would be out of prison by the early 1990s.

Chris was proud of his African heritage. He had been Jan's first choice to replace Mike as Vladimir until Ralph started spreading his venom, trying to portray Chris as a black racist, and stressing that he could not work with him. Jan did not believe what Ralph said about Chris. He told Chris to stop by rehearsals any time he wanted, but for the sake of the play—the bigger picture—he could not have any animosity on stage between those two actors. Ralph went out among the prison population and found Twin, whom he thought he could control. Twin was also black, which Ralph thought would make his actions toward Chris appear less racist. Jan consented and chose Twin.

I was still a silent observer, having known both Chris and Ralph long before the play began. Yes, Chris wanted foremost the best for black people, and he spoke of that in his speech and poetry. He was black and proud, and there was nothing racist or wrong with that. Ralph probably would not have invited any black person to his house for dinner. Yet, I think that Chris and Ralph never liked or gave each other a chance.

Ralph found out that Twin had his own mind, agenda, and aspirations. Ralph could not relate to Twin on stage either. So there was no magic, no truth of the theater, between the two men as Vladimir and Estragon. All this showed on stage during rehearsals like a silver-dollar-sized wart on a baby's face.

Twin was sneaky. I often caught him trying to figure out who I was and what I was doing during the times I was not on stage. Twin and I never hung out as friends. I was from the wide open spaces, and Twin had grown up in the gang-banging territory of L.A. I appreciated Twin on stage, though, because he saw himself as a star and put in the work to become one. On stage, we respected each other and knew that for *Waiting for Godot* to work, we had to be one—one team and one flow.

Ralph became wilder in his assertions of who should be in the play and how the play should be done. But by then Jan, and everyone else, was fed up with Ralph's tirades and demands. Jan had learned a few choice American cuss words and how to deliver them in a black English, Swedish accented, dialect. When Ralph threatened to quit, and told Jan he was starting to sound black, Jan said, "I *am* black, motherfucker. Quit if you want to. This play isn't for you. You can get the fuck out. I am tired of this shit from you about how to perform this play." And that was the end of the first Estragon.

Jan held auditions, this time for a new Estragon. Twin brought in his childhood homeboy, Happy. Jan chose Happy over all the others who came in for the part. Meanwhile Gabriel, the original Lucky, got in trouble and was replaced by Vietnam veteran, J.B. Wells. The last spot filled was the part of Boy. Jan chose a little guy. Danny seemed barely over four feet tall. He had light blond hair and a timid, curious face, just like a real little boy. Jan discovered another prisoner who was a flutist. Finney would sit in a lighted circle on the dark stage at the end of each performance, playing the flute.

Cast set. I played Pozzo, an African man with a white slave and confidante, Lucky. At first there had been four whites and one black, but by the final casting, there were three blacks and two whites. We again sat around

Cast of *Waiting for Godot* at San Quentin, overlooking the garden plaza, 1988.

BEPPE ARVIDSSON

the long table reading the scripts and getting to know each other. We began to merge our different lives and backgrounds into our characters. Happy and Twin, old friends in real life, came across well on stage. The Boy, played by an actor the actual size of a boy, one with boyish ways, came across like a young sparrow exploring the world around him for the first time. Lucky brought life to silence on stage.

Judith had read that Steve Martin, Robin Williams, Bill Irwin, and F. Murray Abraham were going to star in a Mike Nichols production of

Godot in New York, and she wrote to the actors and invited them to San Quentin. Bill Irwin visited two of our rehearsals and gave all the actors advice.

During the later stages of rehearsals, nearly every day someone from Beckett's world showed up to give advice and to see how the play progressed. Theater groups from San Francisco and elsewhere in the Bay Area stopped by; drama students from Stanford, Cal, and San Francisco State came in. Theater folk and directors from France, Sweden, and Austria came by. Some Swedish royalty also visited. Alice Smith, from San Francisco's American Conservatory Theater, volunteered as our stage manager and acting coach. She even trained a prisoner to be assistant stage manager.

The media—local, national, international—was often there to do interviews. The largest radio station in Sweden and the largest Swedish magazine sent journalists to cover our work. I heard that "Good Morning, America" wanted to talk with us. Jan wanted to be somewhat low-key, like Beckett, and he denied many interviews. PBS wanted to film the entire play process, but it fell through because they also wanted an exclusive interview with Mr. Beckett. Beckett and Jan approved an independent film producer, John Reilly, to film some rehearsals, the final performances, and later, an exclusive interview with Mr. Beckett.

Sometime during the last couple of months of development of the play, Jan went back to France to consult with Beckett. He gave the playwright a copy of my chapbook from Judith's class, *No Distance Between Two Points*. Jan told me that Mr. Beckett sat outside in a French café reading my book. Mr. Beckett said, "Good." Then he paused and said, "very good!" He particularly liked the poem, "How Did I Sin?," and repeated the title a few times.

Jan stopped in Sweden and picked up a fine painter, Saga, who was commissioned to paint scenes and portraits of the characters from the play. From across the Atlantic, Saga Linstrom came to America, and she and I met during rehearsals. When I first saw Saga coming into the Education Department at San Quentin with Jan Jonson, our eyes, souls, and hearts met and smiled briefly. I told Spanky, the guy standing next to me, "I am going to marry that woman." At the time I did not know that Saga had read some of my poetry in a pub in Stockholm and that meeting me was one of her reasons for coming to America.

Saga and I would come to see all of humanity—our different cultures and colors—in a child we never had. Even the first day Saga came into San Quentin, we talked naturally, long, and easy about our families, art, lives, and people. We spoke on things we both knew would lead to our being in love. Everything was mysteriously familiar to us, even though Saga came from the other side of the planet and I came from a small town in the desert of California. Saga had been to the Middle East and to parts of Africa. She had traveled across Europe and to some places in Asia. She planned on visiting every continent in the world.

Saga's voice touched my heart and soul in places only moonlight, quiet meadows, sand dunes, hidden valleys, desert cool waters, and singing birds had been able to go. During the rehearsals, when I had on my dark shades, I often could not peel my eyes off Saga until it was my turn on stage. If Saga sat close to me, I would take deep breaths hoping to take her sweet scent back with me to the cell.

Each time I watched Saga leave after a rehearsal, I had a sense of time; I longed for tomorrow, when I knew she would be back. I longed for the rehearsals and for *Waiting for Godot* to never end. My life had meaning. My life had love in the middle of hate, an oasis of trees, grapevines, grasses, and cool waters in the middle of an active volcano. Saga and I kissed a couple of times in the brief moments we found alone in the doorway of the video/music room across from the red brick dungeon walls and rusty metal door.

The infighting between Chris and Ralph, and between Ralph and Jan, and the hating I often noticed coming from Twin towards me—especially when he caught a glimpse of Saga and me talking—was absurd to me. I did not allow the hating to effect me on any meaningful level. Instead, the conflicts gave me time off-stage, moments to whisper to Saga. Besides, I was too busy learning my part in the play; too busy studying Jan, Beckett, Godot, Pozzo, and the rest of the characters in the production; and too busy meeting other artists, actors, directors, and college students to allow the infighting to bring me down. The pure innocence of learning something new each day, indeed, sometimes each moment, made my heart and spirit humble and fertile for growth, like a field in Death Valley flooded with spring rains.

I had lived the play in my silence. I had lived the play ten years earlier in the county jail and during my trial waiting for the death penalty. I had

Spoon just to the side of the door to the red brick dungeon   BEPPE ARVIDSSON
in the basement of the education building, San Quentin, 1988.

lived the play as a little boy hiding under the house and then in the mad-
ness that had brought me to prison. My mom's death and my dad's lack
of words and love were all in the text. The play's magic, Beckett's words,
and Jan's development of the cast became a journey like the odyssey I had
read about in ancient Greek stories. When I happened to see Happy, J.B.,
Twin, or Danny on their way to the chow hall, basketball court, weight
pit, or to a visit or some other function, Beckett's lines naturally came up,
like unforgettable song lyrics.

   Jan was hard on us during rehearsals in the places he needed to be,
inspiring us to touch the depths of truth that can only be found in the
tragedies of ordinary lives and to bring this force to the art we developed.
The pain of doing the text and merging with my character, Pozzo, often
shocked me. But with each tinge of pain, there was growth, pleasure,
and an awareness that I, my life, and things in general would never be
the same. Getting into Pozzo allowed me to embrace a freedom that far
outweighed the pain. The more I let myself go, the freer I became, both
as Pozzo and as Spoon. I was able to go and be in that place—that dusty
road beside a tree that led nowhere, but is everywhere.

   Saga was a free spirit artist, strong, spiritual, and intelligent. She also
possessed the beauty of a Viking princess. During the heaviest times of

rehearsals, when the sense of acting got rough, Saga's glance at me in silence kept me going. Her grace under pressure, and the words we shared when we found a quick moment alone, kept me going. Saga and I often sat silently beside each other. As our souls mingled, she inspired me to act and I inspired her to paint. Saga could be across the room and just her look allowed me to perform a difficult scene. Saga saw me as Spoon, not a prisoner but a human being.

I remember Jan said, "Do the gesture and then say your lines." I remember Alice Smith said, "You must roll, stretch, and lull your words out longer for full impact and clarity on stage." I remember Mr. Beckett wrote silence in this place and that place. I remember Judith said I had a powerful presence on stage, Denise said I had a good voice, and Saga told me that I could do it, to just be myself and the magic would flow.

Sometimes I sat on a stool in one of the soundproof rooms as Saga sketched me. She drew portraits of everyone in the cast, so no one knew of our feelings except our messenger who gave Saga notes and poems I had written. Sometimes Saga sat Indian-style, drawing the cast on stage in the new Arts-in-Corrections building which used to be the laundry room. We started rehearsing there, a more isolated space than the education classrooms. The sound was much better, too. Another cool thing was that there was an upstairs balcony where I could overlook the floor and watch the play develop. I could see everything and be there and not be there. I saw how the rehearsals were filmed. Young college acting and literature students would come upstairs and talk with me. I used to sit on the lip of the balcony overlooking the stage and reflect. I did not want to hide on this balcony like when I was at the new church in the desert. I just wanted another angle to soak in knowledge.

The cast sat for an interview and photo session for a large Swedish magazine in front of the prison chapels by a shallow fountain on the garden plaza. A pair of ducks flew in and landed on the water. Saga was there beside me. The rest of the cast was into the jazz of the interview and photo session. Saga and I were the only ones who saw the ducks. Saga asked me to marry her that moment.

Saga treated prisoners, guards, and free people the same. Everyone was a human being. She did not allow the inhuman rules to dictate her program. Saga stopped and talked with anyone, and the guards did not like this. They often warned her about speaking with prisoners. Saga did not heed their warnings. After some months, prison officials barred Saga from coming back inside. This saddened our hearts, because she did a fine job sketching the characters and the play. But with her banishment, the need to hide our love vanished, and we decided to get married right away.

A week before Saga and I planned to be married, Jim confronted me about our wedding plans. Jim asked me to leave the rehearsal and to go outside to talk.

"Spoon, I think you and Saga should wait until after the play's done before getting married."

"This is my private life!"

"What if you are not allowed to be in the play?"

"Fuck the play."

During the exchange, I felt someone watching me from the art room, and I could see Twin out of the corner of my eye, hovering and listening at the screen door. Word had come to me long before that Twin thought I was in the way of others making in-roads to Saga's heart. There had always been some underlying tension between Twin and me throughout the development of the play, hard feelings that were never expressed, which kept us from becoming friends. I noted his surprise upon hearing that Saga and I were getting married.

Everyone (not only Twin) was shocked to find out that we'd submitted the paperwork and would be married in one week. Some people were mad because they had no idea about us. Some people in the arts program, whom I had known and respected, were mad and disappointed. Love found anywhere, even between cats and dogs or birds and bees, is never an evil or bad thing. None of the arts people offered, or felt it was proper to come to the wedding, though I thought I saw them at other prisoners' weddings. Judith not being there hit me like my arm had been cut off.

Rumors and questions from inmates, guards, arts people, and prison officials filled the air like a sun-rotting pigeon. How could love happen between Saga and Spoon? Why didn't anyone know about their feelings? Why is she marrying him? What does she see in him? She is beautiful and could have any man she wants. Why did she choose a prisoner and a black man?

Apparently I did such a good job playing Pozzo that some prison officials, as well as some of the audience, thought I wasn't pretending and really was like Pozzo. J.B. Wells, who played Pozzo's slave, Lucky, thought this, too. But when I invited J.B. to our wedding as best man, he knew I had only been portraying a character.

The media, and other people from Sweden, were happy for Saga and me. But the people from America—people I had good feelings for—approached me in words, deeds, and silence saying I should wait until the play was over before getting married or I might not be allowed to marry. People I believed in, and who I thought believed in love anywhere, seemed to desert me.

At our wedding, Saga stood in all her Viking beauty in an old grey, floppy, brim hat, a true artist, a painter, with her round glowing face, Grand Canyon big greenish blue eyes and slightly snowy blonde hair. She could have been a model, but she was too much the rebel to stroll for long down a ramp to someone else's beat. We smiled as they pronounced us husband and wife. We smiled because our eyes and hearts shared our own vows in our own ways. We were partners without the paperwork. We got married because it was the thing to do. We could have endured continuous snake-bites to be together, we could endure any ritual, it did not matter.

We went on regular visits and spent every second together, holding hands and living in each other's eyes, souls, and hearts. We could now enjoy each other's voice, kiss, and breath, without having to sneak a kiss or hug like they were something evil or wrong. We could speak of our love aloud and not care who heard. I recited the poetry Saga inspired.

On our family visit, it was like making sweet love for the first time, tasting sugar for the first time, seeing an untouched wilderness valley full of streams and plants. It had been a long time since I had seen such beauty so the moment went too quickly. I barely smelled the tulip.

I was not taught to enjoy the scenery on the trip; for me to get there was the only goal. The second time, Saga came along, and I enjoyed all the colors, flavors, and tastes in the garden. The walk was slow and mindful as well. I lingered in so many places. I studied and pondered the garden, and it really did look like a tulip, a dimpled tulip with its own smell. The sweet rolling hills and thick forest that led to the garden, ripe and bountiful, makes one long to roam around forever. I consciously and lovingly moved about, taking a long time to look and to breathe in and out, mindful of the feel, the texture, the tulip a miracle. The moon hugging the ocean. Our bodies smiled as one.

The next morning we sat on the porch of the family visiting trailer. The sun barely leaned over the walls of San Quentin. We were one—so happy, so loved, so free together. We knew we were love, and within that happiness, we discussed our lives and what the future could hold. "How could they not let you out now, Spoon?" I just looked into Saga's eyes as she continued. "They must let you out now. In Sweden you only do ten years for a life sentence. Don't they see your realness?"

I tried to explain to Saga how it is not about justice or right or wrong in the States, and how a love such as ours is frowned on and often forbidden here, particularly inside prison. We discussed how being together could only get harder, but we believed love could overcome anything: tornadoes, earthquakes, hate, racism, revenge, politics, and politicians. We thought of Romeo and Juliet, and how they went at the apex of their love.

We hoped that eventually some lawyer or group of people would come into our life and share our vision of love, peace, and forgiveness; our vision of painting, acting, prose, plays, and poetry. We thought they would feel and see that what I was convicted of happened a lifetime ago to another, not-yet-awakened soul, that it was like one moment on angel dust. We thought I would get out of prison and that Saga and I would live forever in a village in Sweden with our kids, kids who looked like my niece and nephew, Cindi and Kershon, a beautiful golden brown. The play's development continued, and I could only imagine that Samuel Beckett thought Saga and me being married very Beckettish.

I remember Bill Irwin said to be ready for a let down; he said when the performances were over, we'd face a big let down and a void to fill. I did not understand or see what Bill meant at the time because I had nothing to relate to the end of a performance. But I knew his words were true. I knew when the fall came, like everything else in prison, the fall would be ten times as far and as deep as it would have been in the free world. Bill Irwin could move on to another play, TV show, or some other form of artistry. He could continue a successful run of a play on or off Broadway. But what did I have to look forward to after the last curtain fall of *Godot*?

We had studied the text, rehearsed, and gotten to know the world of Samuel Beckett and *Waiting for Godot* for nearly a year. Now we had reached the final stage of dress rehearsals, interviews, and performances. We performed first before small audiences of Beckett people, theater folks, and prison officials. The first big performances were for other prisoners. We did three performances for them and received as many standing ovations.

The stage was set up in the prison gym. Everything was created and done professionally. The bleachers were packed as we performed *Waiting for Godot* for the first time before an international audience that had come into San Quentin from the outside. We (Pozzo and Lucky) eased around the dark perimeter behind the side curtains. I was nervous, but eager to show a part of Beckett's world, Jan's world, and my world. I stepped on stage, and after a few words, the nervousness melted into timelessness. The silences, bodies, and words on that empty landscape came together and revealed my soul—a universal soul—a happy sad condition of being human. Pozzo and Lucky received standing ovations during our exits. I was in my body, but at times seemed like I was out of it, in a pure state of timelessness.

The heavy luggage of fear and uncertainty the outside audience brought behind the walls evaporated in the heat of the play. The audience joined us on that empty landscape and only honesty mattered. We were no longer convicts in a play. We were human beings, actors with a unique perspective,

Spoon on stage as Pozzo, first act, *Waiting for Godot*, 1988. BEPPE ARVIDSSON

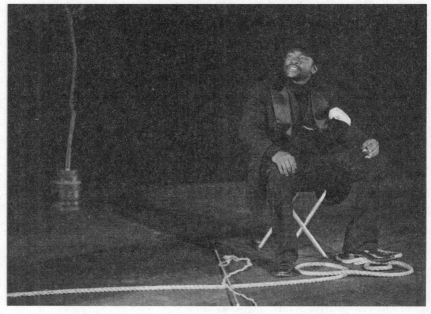

Spoon, Jan, and F. Murray Abraham sharing insights
on performing Pozzo, 1988.   BEPPE ARVIDSSON

able to show the uncut human condition that exists in all prisons of any
kind—mental, spiritual, physical, racial, and cultural.

Many of Beckett's and Jan's friends came to the performances. Beckett's
friend and American publisher, Barney Rosset, and his people were there
from New York, along with a few other *Godot* appreciators from around
the world. Bill Irwin brought his sister. Judith brought her daughter, Sara.
Jim Carlson brought some of his family. Jan's wife, Eva Remos Jonson, an
actress, host, and writer, herself, was there.

Bill Irwin and F. Murray Abraham—who was going to play Pozzo in
the New York production—showed up at one of our performances. Dur-
ing the intermission, Mr. Abraham and I spoke. I found we shared simi-
lar ideas and ways of portraying Pozzo. We both closed our eyes behind
shades in the second act where our character returns blind. Knowing that
a great actor like F. Murray Abraham used the same technique I did gave
me added confidence.

A lot of my special friends and family showed up. My brother, Abe
Jackson, was there plus Saga. And for the friends who weren't able to be
there, their love was present.

113

Beckett's world, Jan's world, Godot's world, and the performances themselves, brought humanity back into my realm. I was no longer in prison. The audience watched human beings, actors, performing a play. The audience saw their own humanity on stage each night. They saw their own feet in light and in darkness, their own dreams, happiness, and sadness. I think those watching knew that to maintain their own humanity, they had to see and feel ours. Our worlds and their worlds were one world expressed in many dimensions.

Still in costume, I came out of the dressing room during intermission on the second night of performance. A poem of mine had been published in the Playbill, so a couple of people from the audience asked me to read some poems. Most of the audience had scattered, taking full advantage of the break between acts. But as I stood between the bleachers reading poetry, the audience began to gather around me. The film crew from New York saw this and began to film my reading. Soon there were about fifty people around me as I read. This audience clapped after each poem. The energy of the reading was heightened by the play's energy, by the theater energy, by the drama of the first act. Only Jan's tap on my shoulder and his words—"Spoon, you must save your voice for the stage!"—stopped my reading.

I have never been so infused, so awakened, so free, and so jazzed with such a mixture of drama and poetry energy since that reading. I could have read poems beyond forever. If I ran out of poems, I figured new poems would have created themselves in the moment like small twisters. Jan brought me back to drama, to Mr. Beckett's poetry, to Pozzo, and to the second act.

We had received long standing ovations after each performance, but I had not seen *Godot* from the audience's point of view in the bleachers. So during the final night's performance, after my exit, still in costume, I strolled behind the bleachers and into an aisle to watch the closing. I heard audience members whispering and looking at me with appreciation. Some patted me on my shoulder. I heard someone say, "There is Pozzo" and another say, "There's Spoon." Their smiles and loving energy were real.

The audience saw *Godot*, they saw Mr. Beckett, they saw Jan Jonson. They saw themselves on stage. The audience saw Pozzo, Spoon, the actor, the poet, the human being not unlike themselves. They saw their reality and interpretation of life on a dusty road, by a leafless tree, on a stage inside prison. But I could now see and feel what Bill Irwin had warned, that big let down. Already, after each performance, when the audience left—after standing ovations, hugs, handshakes, and flowers—the guards quickly moved in and stripped searched the cast.

One mad guard insulted and tried to provoke us after each performance. I remember he came to us, looked at the flowers, and said, "Only women get flowers. You know, bitches. Are you going to take them back to your cells?" So, already, there were let downs after each performance. To be harassed by people did not seem right, not for doing something positive.

Still I stayed pumped up for the next performance. Although that one mad guard kept up his insults each curtain fall, he could not stop the realness, the magic of *Godot* and of Beckett's world. The love and appreciation from the audience and all the folk who knew me and made *Waiting for Godot* work.

Waiting for Godot was foreign to me. I had not known what to expect beforehand, nor did I have expectations. Deep down in my silence, I knew I was human despite anything I had done and the dehumanizing treatment inside prison. But before the play, a lot of my encounters with people—especially from the free world—were as though they were human and I wasn't. Through my involvement in the play, I realized I was still human and folks in non-physical prisons are, too.

When I got arrested and was incarcerated, the impression pounded on me by society and prison was that I ceased to be human because I was convicted of a crime. What makes one inhuman? Mistakes? Ignorance? Being uneducated? Disagreements? Violence? Unenlightened thinking? When did I stop being human? When I was born? Will I again be human once this forced prison time ends?

Godot opened me up to the universe and to an awareness of others, of self, and of life. Poetry woke me up, and drama—the play, the audience, Mr. Beckett, Jan, Judith, Saga, Denise, Jim, Alice, and all the people involved in the production—allowed me to take my body places only my imagination, mind, soul, and heart had been able to go. The entire cast found something they could do in life and it made the world richer and wiser. If I am to believe some of Beckett's people—some media, the critics, actors, artists, and other folks who saw our performances—we could have played on Broadway.

Samuel Beckett watching the San Quentin performance
of *Waiting for Godot* on videotape.

The letdown did come tenfold. It has not let up in over fifteen years.
Knowing that the prison system will not allow the cast to do more plays
is a letdown. Knowing that without a stage and actors, I won't be able to
perfect the plays I have written is a letdown. Not long after the production
of *Waiting for Godot*, I was sent to one of the worst prisons in California,
Folsom State Prison. But we made history with our production, something
that can never be taken away. I still get letters now and then from Sweden,
Norway, and elsewhere in Europe. What I found and uncovered through
my acting, through *Godot*, Samuel Beckett, and Jan, is that prison cannot
touch that realness, love, and the magic of the theater that we created.

11

Cure for Cancer

JAN JONSON, director of the San Quentin production of *Waiting for Godot*, seemed a Cedar Tavern type: brilliant and intense, a phenomenal storyteller who had an "economical with the truth" approach to the facts. In Jan's stories, for example, silent Spoon became a mute man who had not uttered a word for years until the play's inspiration made him willing, as Pozzo, to roar. Jan told us stories about directing *Godot* at Kumla, Sweden's maximum security prison. He gave life to each person mentioned including Kumla's warden, dressed as a Swedish Sinatra, singing "I'll Do it My Way" to his wards. Jan offered a moment-by-moment account of taking his cast to Goteborg to perform, an event that culminated in a mass escape before show time. Those of us listening at San Quentin became an audience of rapt four-year-olds, eyes wide, mouths open, waiting to hear what happened next. Once Jan's performance was over though, once we'd wiped our star-struck eyes, Jim, Denise, and I looked at each other and shrugged with slightly sheepish smiles. *Bravo, bravo;* Jan was without question amazing. But who could possibly discern fact from fiction in his narration?

Jan spun more stories for his San Quentin actors. For weeks before actual rehearsals began, Jan sat with the men he'd selected as cast and built up the story of Vladimir and Estragon. He started with the play's opening line, "Nothing to be done," and painted a picture even those who had never seen a play or read a script could visualize clearly: a "country road and a tree" where two men—with nothing but sore feet, a weak bladder, cold nights, carrots and turnips to eat, endless time, and each other—wait for a Godot who may come that night or, if not, "surely tomorrow."

They wait although they can't quite remember what they have to ask of Godot.

> *Estragon:* A kind of prayer.
> *Vladimir:* Precisely.
> *Estragon:* A vague supplication.
> *Vladimir:* Exactly.

Jan described to his cast what he saw as he walked around San Quentin—a man on the yard hobbling because his state-issued boots were too tight, another in a holding cage with his hands pressed to his belly—and how these scenes reminded him of the play.

> *Vladimir:* It hurts?
> *Estragon: (angrily)* Hurts! He wants to know if it hurts!

He spoke of conversations he overhead in the cell blocks or on the yard that sounded to him straight out of *Godot*.

> *Estragon:* Where do we come in?
> *Vladimir:* Come in?
> *Estragon:* Take your time.
> *Vladimir:* Come in? On our hands and knees.
> *Estragon:* As bad as that?
> *Vladimir:* Your Worship wishes to assert his prerogatives?
> *Estragon:* We've no rights any more?
>
> *Laugh of Vladimir, stifled as before, less the smile.*
>
> *Vladimir:* You'd make me laugh if it wasn't prohibited.
> *Estragon:* We've lost our rights?
> *Vladimir: (distinctly)* We got rid of them.

Jan was shocked when he passed shackled men escorted—the prison word for the action—by guards. "Pozzo and Lucky," Jan pointed out.

"The play is your diary," Jan said over and over to his actors, to visiting drama students, to journalists, and to anyone listening, "The play is their diary."

Jan told the men stories about his visits to Beckett in Paris, describing the café he and the master walked to on boulevard Saint-Jacques and announcing that the playwright kept a copy of Spoon's chapbook of poems by his bedside. Jan talked about visiting Ingmar Bergman at the filmmaker's home on the Swedish island, Fårö, and spoke for hours about Bob Dylan, playing his songs for the men along with appreciative verbal annotation. Jan told of his wife, Eva, who had been the main character on a Swedish children's program similar to Sesame Street. He said that sometimes twenty-year old punks walking down Stockholm streets spied Eva and ran to hug her, calling out, "Eva! You taught me to read!"

Each story Jan spun enlarged and enriched the mostly small worlds the cast members had come from. Jan told the men about Sweden's islands, the country's support for its artists, and the Scandinavian approach to crime and punishment. Jan said, for example, that although a big time drug dealer might get a sentence that lasted awhile, most murderers—murder being the crime least likely to be repeated—were given no more than ten years. I asked Jan if Sweden ever had a death penalty. "Maybe in the 12th century," Jan answered.

Jan had only disdain for the prison rule banning over-familiarity and so he ignored it, flaunted it, or spoke boldly against a rule so inhumane. Which was one of those noble acts that—when seen on the big screen—earns applause from the audience, but which occasioned more muted cheers from those of us trying to make an art program inside a maximum security prison. For we knew from experience that one slip up and the warden might call a halt to the play, kick Jan out, and shut down all of Arts-in-Corrections. Worst of all was that prisoners were the ones likely to suffer most: no more art classes, reduced programming, perhaps being blamed and sent to the hole or transferred. Jim as artist facilitator, Lynnelle and Peter teaching painting and drawing, Aida offering music, all the other teaching artists, and I had learned to make constant, conscious decisions in light of this San Quentin reality.

For me to do my job, for example—for me to teach poetry in prison—I had to manage being familiar without being over-familiar. To be true to the nature of poetry and to the nature of teaching as I understood these, I had to insist of my students, "When you were five, how did your mother walk across the living room floor?" "When you sat on the porch that summer, how did the concrete feel beneath your bare feet?" "How can you make the word 'oppression' in that line come alive in specifics?" "If you could say whatever you wished to your son, what would it be?" I inundated my students with technical information on metaphoric language, direct imagery, rhythm, meter, line break, and such, but if I didn't also ask questions such as, "When you had that talk with your wife, what was she wearing? How did she move her hands?" I would be cheating. In other words, if I didn't discuss the "personal affairs" prison rules prohibited, I would not be doing my job.

But I—all of us working over the long haul—didn't discuss these "personal affairs" in quite the same way we did when teaching elsewhere. In Point Arena, for example, I ran into my extension class students at the Natural Food Store and the elementary school, we talked together about our husbands and children and shared dinner at each other's cabins. At San Quentin, Jim and I spoke often about this. Both our fathers had been college professors, and we were used to a blurrier line between familiar and over-familiar.

I—we all—learned to accommodate the dissonance. Not to "walk the line," exactly, and not to "give in," but to find a way both to follow the rules and, well, to be creative let's say. My diving conversations with Spoon might appear inappropriate, but since they were held in the Arts-in-Corrections office, with the door open and in full view of four associate wardens, few expressed concern. Most Monday mornings, I offered cookies I'd baked to staff, and no authority complained when prisoners stopped by to take one or two from the bag on my desk. When my daughter graduated from high school, she took off to work and travel in Europe. I spent two weeks with Sara in Paris where—in addition to having a fabulous time—I racked my brain for something permitted in the prison to bring back as gifts for my students. Finally I had it. I was allowed to bring in writing material, so I handed out to the men in my class French *cahiers* with postcards pasted on the notebook covers.

I hadn't grown up having to be sneaky to get what I wanted, so my sneaky-skills weren't great, and besides, sneaky made me nervous. Jim and I were alike in this: we were most comfortable letting prison staff know what we were up to, while at the same time, being fairly relentless in pursuing our goals. I called Jim Lieutenant Colombo because he shared with the Peter Falk character a "Sorry to bother you, Sir, I'll get out of your way quick, but while I'm here just let me ask you" approach that disarmed but didn't let up. As for me, I was often compared to a bulldog, albeit one with a smile.

None of which is to say I wouldn't have preferred to talk with Elmo for hours after class, to attend a birthday party for Coties's kids, to give a *Poetry Flash* reading with Spoon, or to take all my students to hear Lucille Clifton when she read at Café Milano. I would have chosen a more open sharing with just about all the men in my class. Still, those few hours each week we had to share poems, and to be as human in each other's company as prison-possible, had value; I wanted those hours to continue. So, although part of me applauded Jan's high drama high road, most of me was concerned.

This concern grew as Jan's work attracted more and more attention. Many on the outside wanted to come into San Quentin and see for themselves. During the months of rehearsal quite a few actors, acting students, photographers, and reporters visited the prison. I rolled my eyes when journalists opened their articles—as nearly all did—by summoning the infamous: Barbara "I Want to Live" Graham, George Jackson, Charles Manson. I seethed when they attributed quotes to Spoon, J.B., Twin, or Happy that clearly, given their wording and cadence, had been spoken by Jan. In every article one cast member or another was made to speak Jan's "this play is my diary" line. I growled at the story Jan told every journalist about Spoon speaking out loud his first words in years in order to be in the play. Jan characterized *Godot* as a primal scream, but for me the scream was the one that stuck in my throat when I read what Jan told reporters.

None of this bothered the cast. Spoon and the others laughed at me for getting so riled up. *Real* was important to most prisoners I'd met, but *truth* was a shakier notion. "Just the facts, m'am" was an approach that had most often been used against them, and so if for once a story misrepresented the truth in their behalf, the men hardly minded.

Of course those who visited *Godot* in production were visiting a maximum security prison and not the Gate Theatre in Dublin. Everything about the project—the creation of prison jobs for the cast that allowed them six months of rehearsal, Jan's free range through the cell blocks, costumes and props brought into the institution, the presence inside of visitors and journalists—was about as unlikely a prison occurrence as could be imagined. Our *Godot* production was one of those Right Place at the Right Time stories, one that involved a new California Department of Corrections director who was serious about both rehabilitation and restitution to victims, and our warden's recognition that he could give his boss both with a production of *Godot* that brought in a large audience invited to make donations to victim services programs. None of what Arts-in-Corrections proposed would have been approved six months earlier—when our desire to develop a controlled poetry connection between Spoon and the children of Point Arena Elementary was squashed—or a year later, when the CDC director was on his way out.

Even in this moment of unusual permission, the presence of each visitor required memos and security clearances written by Jim, Denise, or me. Because we were the contact for those coming in, most thought of us more as staff than as artists—staff in the sense that our job was to do whatever logistical tasks were required to accomplish their goals and staff also in that, for the visitors, we represented the prison and so were the face of repression. Jim laughed most of this off, or, as he put it, he was working so hard he didn't have time to notice that he was being disrespected. I noticed, though, and I didn't like it.

"You're jealous," a friend said when I seethed. I'm sure I was. Jan and his visitors got to be pure artists while Jim, Denise, and I were the plebeian worker ants. Jealous, too, because Sweden might fund creativity, but here in the USA, artists' choices were limited, and all of us working at the prison had to make some compromise to get the rent paid. One could be an artist facilitator like Jim, working forty-hours each week as a Department of Corrections employee in exchange for earning enough money to raise a family, buy a house, and count on some degree of job and retirement security. One could be a contract artist—as Lynnelle, Peter, and I were—with more independence, but never enough money for anything the rest of the world valued. One could work at a job completely unrelated to art-making and paint or write on one's own time. Or one could devote one's life to making art, living of course in that proverbial garret.

I was jealous also because Jan had no problem speaking up for himself and the value of his work, something that was not easy for me. I might be a bulldog in behalf of my students, but I acted more like some scared little puppy when it came to speaking up for my own poems.

Of course I'd been affected by my years at San Quentin as a poet as well as a teacher, citizen, and human being. I'd long kept a writer's notebook, and at the prison, I jotted down bits of overheard conversation, lines that caught my attention, clever phrases, and quick retorts. I was just noting, the writer's equivalent of a visual artist's sketching. After awhile, though, all I saw and heard built up and shaped itself into poems. A process emerged: I imagined a situation—a man in lock up for a number of years, say, never seeing the moon, or a guard waiting for his shift to be over—and then let this being speak in a poem.

The poems piled up, became a long sequence. The form—one imagined voice next to another—made adequate room for my particular way of seeing the world, a vision stated as injunction by filmmaker Robert Bresson: "Accustom the public to divining the whole of which they are given only part. Make people diviners. Make them desire it." I was happy to be writing poems true to this purpose.

But I was also worried. How could I not be? My students were stuck in prison, perhaps forever, and here I was writing poems that made use of the details of their suffering. "Make use of" is one definition of exploitation. Was I exploiting my students' pain for my gain?

When worried or afraid, I tend to go toward what I'm scared of. Besides, I was proud of these poems that, as a sequence, came the closest to conveying my vision of any I'd yet written. So as soon as I had a dozen strong ones, I told my students I'd be our guest artist, and the following week I was. The men paid close attention, but gave me no clue to their feelings until Elmo exploded. I didn't understand what he said, but could tell he felt I'd betrayed him. Chris, new to our class, launched into a well-worded, well-executed tirade: How could I write about their world, which was not my world? Elmo—my ally, my critic, the man I felt closest to in the class—pushed his chair from the table, rose, and walked out of the room.

I couldn't let my voice break or my tears fall. I was the teacher, responsible for the group, and it was my job to get us out of this basement classroom without anyone touching a metaphorical third rail. But where *was* that third rail? My poems, Chris's anger, and Elmo's sense of betrayal were being read by the men in ways I couldn't fathom. Elmo himself is the one who had taught me not to pretend I knew what I couldn't know, so I was aware that I was pretty ignorant when it came to prison racial dynamics and what the men called yard politics. Still, I did realize that these were intense. Elmo and Chris were both strong black men, and I assumed that meant various things to the white, black, and brown men in the classroom.

As did my being a woman. This was 1987. In the outside world, the era of chivalry was over, but inside there were man/woman codes that I ran into daily though they, too, remained beyond my comprehension.

Added to the race, power, and gender issues I didn't understand was the fact that many men in the room had just joined our class after a long lockdown and we didn't yet know each other. Still I was the teacher, and one way or another I had to hold my emotions together for the sake of the group. So though most of my attention was on Elmo out in the hallway—Elmo, whom I cared for so deeply; Elmo, whom I felt so judged by—I took advantage of questions about how a woman could write in the voice of a man and adlibbed a lecture on literature, persona, and imagination.

At home though, I collapsed. Should I stop writing these poems? Should I stop writing altogether? Maybe writing's too dangerous, upsetting people I care for and putting myself in jeopardy. After all, the process of writing this sequence—inviting imagined beings into my mind and letting them speak through me—had lots in common with that blurring of imagination and reality that had made me half-crazy when I was a teenager. Should I tempt fate by courting that state?

One afternoon I talked with Lynnelle, who had been teaching visual art at San Quentin since before Arts-in-Corrections existed. These days she worked on death row. We'd talked often about how best to hold the pain of this place without either becoming rigid or falling apart.

Lynnelle exhibited in galleries, and I published my poems, but no one was banging down our front doors to heap praise or ask for our autographs. I've often heard interviews in which artists are questioned about what they've given up for the sake of their art. Money is usually mentioned, perhaps something about sobriety and decent relationships. Frequently referred to is an out-of-place feeling in a world that values a flush bank account more than spirit and soul. Most of the interviewed artists are fairly well known; the sacrifices these men and women have made live next to their successes.

Lynnelle and I, along with so many others, made the sacrifices without the success. A particular lonely sadness attaches to working hard to shape one's truest vision, foregoing much of what the world cares for, without even validation or recognition. This lonely sadness is one both Lynnelle and I knew well, but what could we do? Lynnelle was sixty to my forty, and we continued to paint and to write because doing so is who we were. We weren't complaining, hardly even commiserating. Still we were both stunned by Jan's confidence, authority, and bravado.

So, yes, okay, I was jealous. But also Jan, and many of the people he brought to San Quentin, forced me to question some of my deepest assumptions. I thought that being blessed with artistic gifts was just that, a gift, one that encouraged gratitude and perhaps even humility. Jan's crowd, however, acted as though thorough dedication to art gave one a pass in the decent person department. One afternoon Jim and I hauled equipment from the art room to the gym where the *Godot* performances would occur. Jim asked Twin, the play's Vladimir, for help carrying something heavy. "I don't have to," Twin pronounced, having picked up on the entitled artist vibe. "I'm a star."

I guess I thought true art making was the kind of work Kate and I did at our separate desks in the country after our children had fallen asleep. That process was quiet, deep, and intense. Jan was certainly deep and intense, but his intensity was loud, communal, and aggressive, whereas Kate's and mine tunneled inward. The difference between theater and poetry, you could say. What I perhaps hadn't realized as a teenager fantasizing about 27 Rue de Fleurus and the Cedar Tavern, but what I was seeing now, was that artists comfortable in settings like those often were not only brilliant, but often boisterous and bombastic as well.

Oh come on, I told myself as I began feeling righteous, aren't you the one who loves Fellini? And I thought of Rojelio—my friend in the country, my performance partner, the one with whom I first visited prison—who often waved his hand dismissively when someone commented on, say, a lovely sunset. Rojelio found beauty as beauty fairly uninteresting. What he hungered after was perception itself and what happened when a human being opened up completely to himself and the world. The art Rojelio demanded I notice was art that resulted from, or encouraged in others, that loud, bloody, unrestrained process.

Whatever my mixed feelings and internal debates, the work that went on in the art room as the cast rehearsed *Godot* was beyond doubt one of the most powerful encounters I've ever witnessed. "They give birth astride a grave, the light gleams an instant, then it's night once more." Is there a line that better conveys our human predicament? Are there people closer to this truth than men serving a life sentence? Jan's overwrought outpourings often caused me to roll my eyes, but Jan was right: in so many ways

Godot was the diary of these men, most of whom had never seen a script before and who now inhabited Beckett's characters with all of themselves.

I felt awe as I watched Spoon become Pozzo, for example. Here was a man, quiet and shy, who summoned the courage to take on the role of a roaring slave master. A poet, Spoon lent his voice to the words of a playwright. A loner who always searched out a spot far from others, Spoon became part of a cast that worked together intensely in a small room for months. In prison, where calling attention to oneself is rarely a smart move, Spoon accepted the risks of being seen. During six performances—three for other prisoners and three for the outside public—Spoon, a man who had explored silence deeply, screamed loudly on stage as Pozzo. Who might Spoon have been, of course I wondered, how might his life have been different, if he'd been given poetry classes and plays to perform when he was a child? Who might Spoon have become if even one elementary school teacher had noticed his gifts?

Many years after my work at San Quentin, a counselor at a juvenile prison told me about a young man who'd been incarcerated at the facility. He read all the books he could find on science and medicine, she told me. He was brilliant. But, the counselor said, this sixteen year old told her he knew that he would be killed by enemies on the street within weeks of his release. And, she reported, he was.

"Dead at sixteen and I wonder," the woman told me, "was that young man meant to be our cure for cancer? He was so serious about science. What new discoveries did the world lose when we lost him?"

I wondered the same about so many of the men I met at San Quentin. Elmo was one of the smartest people I'd ever met, a thinker, journalist, and poet. Who might Elmo have been if he'd learned when young to make maximum use of his intelligence and gifts? Or Coties, with his big heart. Coties might not have been a doctor or lawyer, but he had every capacity to be a great father to his children and the man neighborhood kids came to for encouragement and support. What would he have needed to manifest this outcome instead of a ninety-nine year prison sentence?

My San Quentin students always urged me to keep on working with kids *before* they came to prison, and that's work I never stopped doing. A few years after I taught at Quentin, I shared poetry at a continuation high school. The kids were impressed by my work at the prison and they had many questions. During one conversation, a few of the ninth graders told me they expected they'd end up doing time themselves. I nodded, knowing a few already had records. "Is there anything an adult could say to change that probable future?"

"No," some called out. Then one added, "We each have our own fate."

At that point, 1993, almost all my San Quentin students had been transferred to other prisons. Only Will still remained from our class. Will was one of the few men I'd worked with who was not a lifer; he'd be getting out soon after fourteen years inside. Will had taken advantage of the vocational training programs prisons had at that time and had already been offered two well-paying jobs for when he got out. I visited Will and asked him about what the continuation high school students had told me.

"They're right," he said. "I wouldn't listen to anyone when I was their age, either."

I must have looked hopeless.

"But," Will added, "adults never stopped talking to me, planting seeds. And when it was time for those seeds to sprout, they did, even though I was in prison. I doubt I'd have been able to make the changes I made if no one had planted those seeds."

I took this seed image back to my high school students and they nodded. They talked about the positive messages adults gave them and the value these had even though the good words didn't change their behavior.

"We need adults who make sure we know that they care," the students told me.

I asked the class to make lists of the seeds they felt had been planted within them and then asked them to imagine who they might be years down the road when it was time for these seeds to crack open and bloom. Each high schooler made a collage and we pinned these to the wall.

The youngsters seemed to be asking adults to help them hold hope—to be a source of encouragement and passionate concern—and simultaneously to detach, to set the youth free to follow their fates. Perhaps this is what teenagers have always asked of adults, but I knew, and the teenagers knew too, that the stakes were higher in our era when guns were used instead of fists or knives and prison sentences grew longer and longer.

In *Father Greg and The Homeboys,* a book that came out during the years I taught at the continuation high school, author Celeste Fremon described Father Greg Boyle's work with Latino gang kids in East L.A. as "lighting a pilot light." She wrote that Father Greg often had to relight each pilot many times before the light stayed on.

One of my favorite Spoon lines goes, "As human beings, we all have one foot in light and one foot in darkness." I've never read a better description of this human truth. One can argue about nature or nurture, karma and fate, economic inequity and social injustice. But whatever the reasons and roots, I was sure there were men at San Quentin who might have found "the cure for cancer" if life had early on helped them nourish that one foot in light.

12

Banished

I HAD BEEN BANISHED from San Quentin, the art world Mecca of California prisons with its classes in acting, juggling, visual arts, book binding, animation, music, drumming, and film making, along with the outside artists who came in to teach, grow, share, and learn. Banished from one of the few California prisons that still had a college program; from a data processing training that had been featured on CBS News; from religious programs that brought people from the free world together with prisoners and welcomed me, a sometimes pagan; and from my new friends and family in the Bay Area. The State even wanted to banish me from being in love and being loved. The California Department of Corrections wanted to ban me from my Swedish wife, Saga. The powers that be ultimately wanted to ban me from walking in realness and wanted me only to stroll in angry silence and madness.

Even before I left San Quentin for Folsom, there had been a slight break in the flow between Judith and me when I was not allowed to correspond with the young people from Point Arena Elementary School. This was a breach that deepened, shook, and squeezed my heart and soul. At one point, Saga and Jan had convinced me that Judith no longer had my best interest at heart. They told me that I should secure all of my poems back from Judith, as she kept my poetry in her file cabinet in the Arts-in-Corrections office. I did almost take my poems back, especially after Judith refused to come to my wedding. I guess she thought it would be a conflict of interest, which made me think that perhaps she did not believe in me or the love and happiness I could find despite being in prison. I saw no concern from her I could feel.

Now banished to Folsom, I told myself that I did not need or want Judith's advice on my work. I thought San Quentin was the past and just a phase on my journey. It was as though Judith was on one side of a deep, rushing river and I was on the other. I had to put distance between us, and I refused to write Judith for a long time and ignored the photocopied form letters and poems she sent from a Department of Corrections approved formal address.

What had I done to be banished? All I had done at San Quentin was to educate myself, from the inside out, and to find out that I was a poet, writer, and actor. I discovered I had something positive to offer, and that it was better to build up than to destroy, better to love than hate, better to live than die, better to grow than vegetate. I learned that it took more courage not to kill than to kill, more strength to be a peaceful leaf floating on the waters than a tumbling brittle leaf crumbling on dry ground. Why was I banished from a poetry class that had enabled me to find my gift, what I did best in life? Why was I banished?

I stepped off the bus at Folsom Prison, handcuffed and shackled around the waist, hands, and legs. There were correctional officers on both sides of me, both of them black. At the time, we were still allowed to smoke cigarettes, and I had managed to light one before descending the bus. The cop on the left got into my face and said to put out the smoke. For a moment, I wanted to hurl the cigarette along with spit into the officer's eyes. The warder on the other side of me said, "Are you going to let him tell you what to do?" and that brought me to the reality of what was happening. I must have had f-o-o-l written all over my forehead. These men wanted to set me up. If I acted out, I would have been left with missing teeth, broken bones, a good ass-kicking, plus a charge of assault on staff, even though I would have been the one provoked and assaulted. What chance would I have had to win such a fight even if I were not handcuffed, chained, and shackled like a transported slave?

The transfer was unreasonable and unbelievable. After finding my niche as a poet and writer, after the successful run of *Waiting for Godot*, how could I be sent to a worse prison? San Quentin staff had gone through the motions of clearing me for a lower level prison, but they ignored their own clearance and sent me on the first bus to Represa, California: Folsom Prison.

At my initial classification hearing, committee members read my file and said that I should start some kind of drama program at Folsom, but they offered me no way to do so. They also said I was cleared for a Level III placement, according to a report in my file. The committee pretended to be puzzled about why San Quentin did not follow through on that transfer to a lower security prison.

Old timers at San Quentin had told me that everyone should experience Folsom Prison and learn some respect. They said Folsom was a place where you will lose your girlfriend or wife, your family and friends, perhaps even your life. They said Folsom Prison was a set up to fail.

I was sent from orientation at New Folsom to Old Folsom. I thought, since Old Folsom was as old as San Quentin, it must have positive programs for self-restoration so at first I was glad to be sent there. At San Quentin, I'd always been single celled. Having a cell to myself was important to me. But to stay at Old Folsom, I would have to waive my single cell rights. Still, under the illusion that Old Folsom would have as productive an atmosphere as San Quentin, I agreed to sign these rights away.

The cell blocks were almost the same as at San Quentin except Old Folsom tiers seemed longer, lonelier, deader, more sinister, and darker, as if less sunlight or moon light or light in general lived there, less life and hope. And the old timers were right: there were no programs, hardly any jobs, and no self-help groups at Old Folsom. Staff set my custody level higher than it had been at San Quentin. When I protested through the paperwork channels, I was told: "This is the warden's prison and he can set the custody as he pleases."

As if all that wasn't bad enough, the entire yard was half the size of a football field, and prisoners could not walk or sit on the grass inside the tiny circle at the yard's center. Prisoners could only walk in one direction around the track. I wondered why I had allowed New Folsom staff to send me to Old Folsom. An old rock church stood at the top end of the yard. Only a few elite people were allowed to attend this church. There was also a nice library that we could hardly ever get into.

The basketball court sat in the middle of the walkway right next to Cell Block One. Beside the block were tables where prisoners played cards and dominoes. Everything was hideously crowded. During basketball games, hundreds—perhaps even a thousand—prisoners walked to and fro and one could get beat down, stuck, or killed. No one would see you lying there injured or dead, not for a long time.

The weight pile was embedded into the side of a small rock hill. There was one entry and exit point through a barred metal turnstile which reminded me of the gates and crowded pathways cattle run through in slaughter houses. The weight pile, or pit, consisted of free weights, dumb-bells, and twenty-five pound metal quarters placed on long bars on bench press benches. The pile was like a big sunlit cave that had workout benches grouped in sections by race or gang. The dumbbells ranged from 10 to 150 pounds and the bench press bar went up to maybe 500 pounds. I was known for the depth of my chest and the horseshoe of my back arms. We were locked into the pit and let out on the hour. Clung on the cliff, overlooking the weight pile, was a guard shack, and often when something happened or did not happen in the weight pit, the officers shot indiscriminately. There was no room in the pit for uninvolved prisoners to get out of the way.

In 1989, Folsom was an end of the line prison. I did not care for Old Folsom at all. When I asked why there were no programs and no protests and why things were lifeless, hopeless, and dead, most prisoners said, "This is Folsom, man!" over and over again. "This is Folsom, man!"

The more I moved about Old Folsom, the more I began to die inside. I felt myself crusting over, felt hope and love seep out of me as though I was a tire slowly going flat. I knew if I stayed at Old Folsom, I would die there like the rest of the zombies strolling around the yard pretending to be alive. I felt the hopelessness in the air and it fumed like a mountain of fresh shit.

No, I did not care for Old Folsom at all. So when the counselor came by the cell to get my signature on the papers that would sign away my single cell rights so that I could stay at Old Folsom, I declined. He reminded me of the agreement we'd made but I said, "I don't recall making any such statement."

The counselor left that day thinking that I would come to my senses. He believed that Old Folsom was better than New Folsom. He thought he would give me some time to pine things over. Two weeks passed and the counselor came back to the cage. "If you don't sign the waiver, you will be sent to New Folsom B Facility."

Again I said, "I don't recall making any such statement." The counselor walked away, and I began advising other prisoners coming from San

Quentin not to sign away their single cell rights either. The next day I was walked back across the road to New Folsom, B-Yard. Staff, administration, and prisoners kept conflicts—gang and racial violence—active on B-Yard, on more than one occasion deemed the most violent prison yard in the state of California.

Yet I preferred to be there among the wayward prisoners, staff, and administration immersed in violence and long lockdowns than to be at Old Folsom, imprisoned and dying in hopelessness and despair. There were no programs at New Folsom, either, but at least the cells and the yard were much bigger. There were no Keep Off the Grass signs at New Folsom and there were two full-court basketball areas, a gym, and an unfenced weight pile. The church and library were more open, too.

Saga, my wife, had to commute many miles just to visit me. Being from Sweden—the other side of the planet, a country where basic human needs are met and the arts and restorative justice are appreciated and promoted—Saga found herself lost and disillusioned by America's money-before-people system. Everything became more difficult. Once she was mugged while on a bus in San Francisco after visiting me.

Saga tried to get me out of prison. I had at least 100 pounds of court transcripts and she hauled these to a prominent appellant attorney who gave her free advice. Saga somehow found the same lawyer my family could not afford eleven years earlier, long before I had met her. The lawyer even remembered my case. He perused the court papers briefly and suggested that a point of attack might be that I had an all white jury. I considered the idea, but knew I'd need a lawyer and money to fight, research, and flesh out the litigation.

Not long after I arrived on B-Yard New Folsom, the big prison riot between Southern Mexicans and African Americans took place. [Editor's Note: The prison term "Southern Mexicans" originally referred to Mexican Americans from Southern California who run as gangs.] One morning I noticed that there were no white prisoners on the yard. I knew something was up, but I was not going to miss yard. The upper basketball and handball courts were both just above the weight pile where the Southern Mexicans hung out. There were hundreds milling around in winter coats in the middle of hot weather as though they were in a park in East L.A.

I was walking the track with an Islander. We had just cleared the Southern Mexican area and were standing on the far side of the gym when I noticed a Southern Mexican now stood next to me and looked back up the hill to his people. Then—boom—the yard exploded: dust, fists, and knives flew everywhere. The entire yard, hundreds of prisoners, were locked in battle while the guards shot from the yard and the cell block towers. One black prisoner—back in prison due only to a parole violation—was shot and killed.

It took me about a minute to deal with the Southern Mexican who stood next to me. We rolled on the ground and separated as the bullets, dust, rocks, and knives flew. I was fully conscious of what was still going on around me. Most of the combatants, some bloody with knife and bullet wounds, had dropped to the ground. Some of the biggest guys, and the ones who talked the most shit on the yard, ran, while some of the smallest guys stood and fought like gladiators. When there was a lull in the battle, some Southern Mexicans jumped back up from the ground and tried to attack black prisoners still laid out in the dirt. Some of the attackers were hit by gunfire for jumping up and some blacks—hipped to the trick—bounced up to meet the attack.

In my fight, I ended up down close by the prison library. I heard prison staff say, as they rushed out of the Watch Office, "I knew this was coming. I knew this was going to happen. What took it so long?"

They separated us by skin color, handcuffed and stripped us down naked. It took them hours to get all prisoners to the cells. I had known the Southern Mexican who tried to stab me from back at San Quentin. We had been in a couple of self-help groups. We fought as though we were strangers.

I had not known this kind of racial hatred between blacks and browns until I came to prison. I had grown up with Southern Mexicans in the heart of the high desert, on Crooks Street, close to the river bottom. We had crossed the field and gone to school together and we ran up and down the dry river past Blacks Bridge. We released hogs from pig farms along the way. We had rock fights against hobos and other kids and hooked pigeons with clothes hangers from the metal and wooden pillars of the long bridge that ran over the rail yard near "B" Hill. We took long bike rides and went bottle- and jackrabbit hunting for food. We rode slow moving trains to Ferguson Park for baseball practice and games and sometimes stole and shared candy bars along the way from corner markets.

Blacks and Southern Mexicans grew up like brothers on Crooks Street. Andrew, Felix, Raymond, Barney and Frankie Saiz, Clyde Barrila, Bucky,

Willard, Willie, Mack, Leon, Robert, Turkey, R.T., Danny and Randy Yabor my half-brothers. We all had run together and grew up goosing girls in school and playing hide-and-go-get-it with the older girls, Peggy Love and Mary Birdy. We did not see black or brown. I saw food when I went over to Isaac Plata's house for tacos, beans, tortillas, and Mexican bread. We were the River Bottom boys from Crooks Street and we left our doors and windows open. We stood together in elementary school on the playground when I locked the white Mr. Williams in the basement.

And now here I was on the ground at New Folsom, having fought people I had grown up with as family. Brown people who still asked my brothers Abe, Bishop, and Terry about me even over twelve years after I'd been in prison.

What is this shit? I thought, ready to die in a prison riot.

Meanwhile Saga waited in the visiting room for me to come see her. The prison officials told my wife and the other visitors that there had been some trouble on the yard. The visitors had heard all the shooting, but the prison officials did not even tell them if their fathers, sons, brothers, or husbands were dead or alive. Even weeks later, long after the riot was over, no word. They just said, "No visiting, go home."

I could only sit in the cell thinking about how it had been at San Quentin. I remembered that one teacher there, the video instructor, had told me that when *Waiting for Godot* was over, I would be just another inmate again. I had never verbally or physically abused this man, but he was envious and jealous of all the attention the cast of *Godot* received during the play's development.

Even before *Waiting for Godot*, before I met and married Saga, when I went to other programs like A Course-in-Miracles, I observed the video teacher watching me as I conversed with women from the free world— teachers, guest artists, journalists, or volunteers. I believe women are to the world what the stars and planets are to the universe. I did not allow the bars to alter much how I wooed or courted a woman, whether in person or through the mail.

I had not thought that the video instructor watched me with hateful or jealous eyes, although there were other prisoners and staff who watched, hated on, and disliked me for the same reason. How splendid life would be if people spent the time given to hating on others to working instead on themselves and enhancing their own walk on this planet.

The video teacher, in one of his polite or confused moments, told me that his taste in women was the same as mine. He spoke right after he saw me speaking with my lovely lawyer friend, Katherine Greenwood. I had never discussed my taste in women with him.

Women have written me that one of their fantasies has always been to be with a man in prison. Yet, often when the reality of incarceration hits them—after weeks, months, or years—the fantasy, the dream, festers and fades like dark clouds in Death Valley.

One time, someone turned me on to a girl who lived in Portland, Oregon. We exchanged a few letters and phone calls. In no time, our relationship became vibrant, sweet, and heavy. At one point, I wrote Veronica fifty-page letters—front and back: hundred-page letters. I cannot remember anything we talked about except love and making love, dreams of being together eternally.

Veronica began to fly down from Oregon to visit. We believed we could do whatever it took to stay together. One evening I called and Veronica's daughter, Destiny, answered the phone. I asked to speak to her mom and Destiny told me, "She's with her boyfriend."

"Boyfriend?"

By this time Veronica had taken the phone. I could hear a man's voice in the background as she spoke in tears. I cried inside my heart. Veronica was cool, thick, sexy, and spirited as an Arabian filly. I still hoped our relationship was not over, but it was. We visited twice more after the phone call. We still had feelings, love, for each other, but the fire had changed course and our paths parted. I could not go to Blacks Bridge to begin to heal my heart as I had done in the free world. I could only go deeper within myself.

More than one woman has left me in the years I've been in prison. Not because there was no love, but because there was no ultimate love-making—no sex. No rolling over into sweet woodlands in the middle of the night or at dusk or dawn. No grasses to cushion our footfalls. How could I blame Dorothy, Veronica, Yaro, Eva, Briana, or Annie for moving on? How could I hold them hostage to love that cannot be physically fully expressed? I cannot be mad at any of those brilliant and beautiful women who opened my life, each in her own way.

I suppose the video teacher back at San Quentin got a kick out of watching me to see who I spoke to. It was a shame and it blew my mind how often people who did not even know me, people who had never even spoken to me, hated on me—free staff, guards, and other prisoners. Some hateful prisoners tried to get other inmates to attack or provoke me. Even an outside filmmaker who came into San Quentin smiled in my face as he shot footage on *Godot*, and then at parties outside the prison hit on my wife, Saga.

Some correctional officers hassled Saga because she was Swedish, beautiful, and white, while I was African, black, and proud. The prison system's rules were anti-love, anti-forgiveness, anti-family, anti-visits, anti-humanity, and anti-relationship, particularly between people of different skin color. Saga was alone in a hypocritical America of which California's prisons were only an extension. All this caused problems for Saga, as though someone was tossing fist-sized rocks above her head and watching them fall. The struggles against the system became painfully etched over Saga's face. Each time she left after a visit, she felt like her mom or some other loved one had died.

Saga was not a big woman and she had started to lose weight; the white chocolate luster of her skin dimmed like a winter sunset. My mouth and mind began to tell her to go back home to Sweden, but at the same moment my eyes and heart told her to stay. I said, "Go home, Saga, Baby, it's cool," and she would come back with, "I can handle it, Spoon, *Jag älskar dig*."

Saga wanted to stay in America and be with me and I wanted her to stay. But we both knew she must go; she must go to keep her mental, spiritual, and physical health. The American system, that inanimate object, doesn't appreciate realness or love much, or feelings governed by the heart. Saga had to go to be in her own light and to live her own life.

It took Saga a while to find out if I was dead or alive after the riot. During the long lockdown, and still in the midst of the on-sight war which required that any time a black and Southern Mexican came in contact or in sight of each other they had to fight, the prison started up family visits again. On family visits, prisoners are allowed two nights and days with family members in apartments inside the prison complex. As I arrived at the family visiting area, another cop escorted a Southern Mexican to the same corridor. The prisoner and I stared each other down, but did not take off. The officers who had escorted us must have known there was an on-sight war going on and a no mixing of the races policy. But the man and I did not attack each other, and we each went on to enjoy our family visits with our wives.

At the end of the family visit, the officers brought me and my wife Saga, plus the Southern Mexican prisoner and his wife, to the same good-bye area. Again the Southern Mexican and I stared at each other, though not as fiercely as we had on our way to our visits. In silence we agreed not to fight. After our wives were led away to the free world, the guards looked into the good-bye area as if they were in a panicked state. They separated us, asking how did a black and a Southern Mexican end up in the same holding area, since the two groups are at war and under separation orders.

The lockdown lasted a few months. On our last visit I felt in my soul, and saw in Saga's eyes, that she was leaving. She told me that if a train is headed for a wreck and you know it is, you must get off. I agreed. In my mind, and some hidden part of my heart, I gave her my blessing.

Saga and I are forever friends, but we have gone on with our lives, are no longer married, and are separated by an ocean. I still believe in love as swans do. I still love and sometimes get love back. But there is an ever-present layer of sadness running through love, like the underground river in the Mojave Desert. I know love and realness is in all situations, sometimes hidden like a white rabbit on a snow-capped ridge. Love inspires every word in this story. If one gives love and forgets it, love comes back in tidal waves. And yet, I don't know.

There was a lake Saga and I went to every night at ten o'clock. We met in the sky as seagulls. There was a big rock lakeside where she sunbathed. To see Saga unclothed and tanned was like eating saltwater taffy. We had our own suns, moons, and grasses, however we wanted them. The lake: our place of love and realness—an oasis between, above, and beyond the prison walls. Diana, flowing in her silk nightgown, watched us move in the high grasses like bird wings, gliding on air, flapping now and then. When the rough winds came we dipped, we paused, until we found the warm pockets of dark sweetness, until we found a breeze to rise again. Love is easy and hard. No love is ever lost, though it sometimes transforms and moves on in the moment like heavy clouds. I felt loved all those moments we were together.

When I discovered poetry in 1986, I did not know the passions, emotions and new worlds that would meadow my life and path. I did not know a graveyard of pains often twins or follows mountains of love.

13

Write Reckless

SEPTEMBER, 1988 and rumor had it that San Quentin would soon change from a maximum to a medium security prison. We'd heard these rumors before, but now rumor quickly became fact: men walking the yard one day vanished the next. Spoon—who'd had the courage to go against prison instinct and call attention to himself in *Godot*—was one of the first to be transferred. He sensed he'd be gone shortly after the play was over, and then overnight, he was. No Spoon in class, no Spoon in the spiral staircase, no Spoon at the office door wanting to talk. Only a note from Spoon left on my desk:

> Thanks for helping me tremendously to open up and express the light in me. Before you I was only able to outwardly express the dark side of me. I am not making a judgment that dark is bad and good is light.
>
> But now I am just expressing more of the real side of me and the growth in me. I care for you still as my sister in some ways. And definitely as my mentor. I care about you as a friend.
>
> There's much more you could have helped me with and I meant to say goodbye but would have gotten too emotional. It feels like I need you in my life cause you know what you are. We still need to say goodbye proper though. I still want you in my life!

Me, too. I wanted Spoon in my life, though it's true, we'd just gone through a rough patch. Working hard on *Godot* had in no way been part of my job. I'd known why I was putting in so many unpaid hours—the play and the process were amazing—but I was often pissed off, especially at times like when I felt Spoon test me over his wedding. He'd said nothing to me about the ceremony, hadn't asked me to attend, and the message I heard in his silence was: Do you care enough to show up despite Saga's rudeness, my distance, and the fact that I haven't formally invited you?

Because Saga had been allowed into the prison through Arts-in-Corrections, their love—hers and Spoon's—threatened both the program and the play. Jim, responsible for both, told me he wasn't going to the wedding. He preferred I didn't either, but said it was my call.

I'd spent my years at Quentin trying to honor that Robert Bresson quote about divining the whole of which we're given only part. Elmo frequently pointed out that my hunger for wholeness was a luxury no prisoner could afford. He said that he lived in a partisan world and had to make choices. Now I did too. Was I going to attend Spoon's wedding or wasn't I? As the moment approached, I felt much closer to Jim, more loyal; we were working so hard, shoulder-to-shoulder, in the service of *Godot*. Still, though Spoon had lately been cold, I knew what he and I shared.

Spoon called me his big sis and the image of tall, thin, dark-skinned Spoon next to short, round, freckly me made me smile. He also called me his mentor, an honor, though one I accepted with a tinge of discomfort. "Equality" was the banner flown during my coming of age; was it okay to be someone's mentor? Big sis, mentor, Spoon. So should I walk over to the visiting room for the wedding or shouldn't I? That morning found me enmeshed in a film crew's demands, and by the time I looked up at the clock, I knew that the ceremony was over.

Spoon's test had annoyed me, but bottom-line, I'd failed that test. The failure was less not showing up and more not making my own clear decision. In the epigraph to his poetry chapbook, Elmo had quoted Martin Luther King Jr.: "The ultimate measure of a man is not where he stands in moments of comfort and convenience, but where he stands at times of challenge and controversy." Spoon had made attending his wedding a challenge, but I knew that I'd taken the easy way out and that I measured short.

Spoon stopped talking to me. "Give me back your copies of my poems," he spit from the spiral staircase as I passed a few days after the wedding.

"You mean that? After all these years, you mean that?"

I insisted we talk, and it didn't take long before we were both in tears.

And now Spoon was gone. Although I wanted Spoon in my life, I still worked under Arts-in-Corrections, and the prison rule against over-familiarity continued to govern my actions. I couldn't write full letters to Spoon, couldn't visit him, or accept collect phone calls. Despite the deep human connections that had encouraged Spoon to develop the best in himself, prison deemed human connections dangerous and therefore forbade them.

The only active thing I was allowed was to send poems, so I mailed off solace in the way that I could. Poems had opened the door to Spoon's recognition of the niche he now knew was his. We all—Spoon, I, and every San Quentin poet—had worked to build poetry into a vehicle sturdy enough to provide sustenance during hard times. Still, I knew that any poem I sent in the mail could provide only flimsy support given the force of the shove that pushed Spoon from the heights of *Godot* to the depths of New Folsom.

That September began my last year on the grant I'd been awarded and I was in the mood for some solace myself. My time at the prison was running out at the same moment that many of my students began to be transferred elsewhere; Jim left Quentin that month to work as assistant manager for all of Arts-in-Corrections; Lynnelle suddenly died. And it was then that Sara took off for work and travel in Europe. September 1988 was one sad, lonely September.

With one bright spot. Bill Cleveland, state-wide manager of Arts-in-Corrections, hired me to research and write a manual for artists working in prison. Although Elmo and Chris had been troubled by the poem sequence I'd written during my years at San Quentin, Bill appreciated the work and my effort to see from multiple perspectives. The longer I worked at the prison, the more I saw. In my first year—the year of our once-a-week class—my attention had focused almost completely on my students as individuals and on the group that we formed. When given the grant that let me be on-site for twenty hours each week, I learned more about the context in which my class existed: wardens and associate wardens; secretaries and free staff; guards and the variety of ways that they guarded; memos, clearances, gate passes, and the chain of command; West Block, South Block, East Block, and North Block; the five tiers of each cell block, officers patrolling from gunrails, the open showers and mildew, catcalls, and the cry of gulls through the vaulted glass that seemed not to have been washed since the nineteenth century when the prison was built.

Bill valued my curiosity and interest in point of view. He wanted me to write the manual using a shifting lens and to approach the bulk of the book, not as a reporter, but as an artist. We talked about what this might mean and came up with the idea of a novella told from multiple points of view. My first task was to travel to many of the state's prisons (then slightly more than one dozen) and to interview prisoners, teaching artists, community resource managers, wardens, and line staff to learn about their responsibilities, thoughts about prison and prisoners, and experience with Arts-in-Corrections. Therefore, by the night of our last San Quentin class the following June—my grant period over, many of my students already transferred—my awareness of prison had rippled far outward from the walls of our classroom.

During that last meeting, in the midst of the closest thing to a party I could get permission to create, Elmo—my primary debate partner on point of view matters—surprised me with a perspective about-face. Elmo said, "Now *I'm* going to give *you* an assignment. Write about these past four years from *your* point of view. Tell us *your* story, let us know what *you* learned."

Did Elmo, who had serious issues with my Quentin poems, intend a friendly barb or was this a sincere suggestion? I wasn't sure, but over the following days I thought a lot about Elmo's assignment. I hadn't intended to write about my years at San Quentin beyond the poems and few essays I'd written while working there. Still, all those writer's notebooks I'd filled with overheard phrases were stacked on my bookshelves and without doubt the four years I'd spent at the prison had been among the most important in my life. Besides, I had such a good story to tell: trips to the cell blocks during a lockdown; a visit from a Nobel Prize winning poet; *Godot* at San Quentin; Elmo's fierce intelligence, Coties's caring heart, and Spoon's discovery of himself as a poet; all those relentless lessons provided by prison paradox. Most important of all, I had just experienced a world hidden from most everyone's sight. I'd shared poems for four years with men many thought of as the embodiments of evil. But my students weren't evil, no matter the crimes for which they'd been convicted. They were human beings with "one foot in light and one foot in darkness." I felt something like a moral duty to make that simple truth public.

So I began writing. I knew I wasn't going to convince anyone with facts and statistics since even when I learn such details they don't remain in my brain. No, what I had to share were stories, my deep feelings for the men I'd worked with, and the images that arose the moment I sat down to write: the shadows barbed wire casts, the arched entrance to West Block with its latticed metal gate, Mount Tamalpais out the back window of the education building, the puncture-resistant turtle-shell vest that staff insisted I wear when I went to see students in cell blocks, Jai Siripongs' drawings from death row, apt sayings (*Never call your cell home; it's not your home. If you come back to a cell that's been ransacked, be glad. Let it remind you: never get too comfortable here*), the ferry returning from Larkspur to San Francisco as it sailed by the prison, walking into the prison along a path that placed death row on my left and the Catholic chapel on my right.

I saw, heard, noticed, and recalled, but my writing was labored. Elmo had been clear: "Write about these past four years from your point of view." But point of view is a function of where one is positioned, and I couldn't see clearly from where I was standing for I was too close to the years I'd just lived. I could describe scenes and tell a few stories, but couldn't find ground at far enough distance to make these stories and scenes work.

Besides, I missed my San Quentin students, scattered now all over the state. I wrote notes and sent poems. Though I no longer taught at the prison, I did continue to work for Arts-in-Corrections—finishing the manual Bill had hired me to write and creating a newsletter for the program—and so remained subject to the over-familiarity rule. Spoon, Elmo, and Chris let me know that if I wasn't going to write all the way real, why bother to write at all? I—point-of-view queen—understood how they felt, but refused to let go. I wrote the men that I'd continue to send what I could whether they wrote to me or not, and that's what I did.

When I was finally able to write to my former students simply as Judith, Spoon wrote right back. We must have written over one hundred letters that year when we were, as Spoon put it, finally "human to human, with only the mental prisons to burst through and grow from."

I wrote Spoon about how I'd seriously considered giving up the work I so loved at San Quentin when the prison wouldn't let him keep the poems of the Point Arena children. He responded: "I knew you and Jim wanted me to be able to write the kids back. I didn't know that you thought I was right (I use that word under protest) about the situation. You never told me so. I also didn't know that you wondered if you were wrong to continue working there. I believe you made the correct choice."

Judith and Spoon in the visiting room
at CMC, mid-1990s

VISITING ROOM PRISON
PHOTOGRAPHER (POLAROID)

Spoon made his own admissions: "You probably know I have always been selfish towards you—meaning I wanted you only to myself, only to be with me helping me with my writing and my helping you with yours."

Although Spoon was at California Men's Colony now—in San Luis Obispo, over two hundred miles from San Quentin—in some ways I felt closer to him than when he sat in the spiral staircase or our classroom. At the prison, there had always been so much going on. When we sat in the Arts-in-Corrections office, part of my attention was on Jim's 'phone call or on the associate warden across the hall walking our way. In the classroom, there were so many men—and the men as a group—to track. Standing outside Spoon's cell in West Block, I could sense the officer behind me on the gunrail and the man down the tier flashing a mirror trying to see just who it was near his cage. Now, in my apartment, sitting in my rocking chair reading Spoon's letters, I could focus. Spoon's voice in his letters burst with an enthusiastic energy— the plays he was reading! the poems he was writing! this prison dedicated to programming! In my mind's eye, I could easily see Spoon on the bunk in his cell, reading a letter from Saga in which she let him know that Jan had met with Bob Dylan and had shown the songwriter Spoon's poems; at a desk in a prison classroom, writing a play; sitting by a light pole on the yard, reading Shakespeare. "Are you smiling now?" Spoon asked every few pages.

I was, which was rare at that time. Sara was far away in Europe and when she came back, she began college. A relationship with a man I'd loved a great deal had just ended. My efforts to write the book Elmo suggested weren't working. The Gulf War was underway and a major recession on the horizon. And then a letter arrived from Elmo at Tehachapi, the prison to which he'd been transferred. Chris had been transferred to Tehachapi, too, and Elmo wrote—carefully, warning me about bad news—that Chris had been killed in a cell fight. Chris had always told us that the stars promised he'd be out of prison by the early 1990s and now he was. The poems I wrote in those months formed a long sequence, one I titled, "In the Crook of Grief's Arm."

Spoon signed most of his letters with the words *Write Reckless*. The truth, though, was that I was less reckless than wrecked, for I was being hit by a bout like the one I'd undergone when I began college. Spoon encouraged me not to sink. He offered analysis—I did too much for others, and not enough for myself—as well as the observation that perhaps depression is more usefully thought of as growing pains. Mainly he did what he could to hold up for me the mirror I had held for him, the one in which it's possible to see one's own kindness, generosity, and spirit, and not only that one foot in darkness.

Still I was sick—depression, migraines, hallucinations. I could not summon adequate stamina both to earn money for rent and to finish the book about my years at San Quentin. I had few resources, but also almost no responsibilities, and I considered my options. Sara was grown and gone and I could take off: travel to Paris, join the Peace Corps or Mother Teresa, move back to the country. Instead, what I packed up were the chapters I'd written, along with my notes. I put everything in a box, which I hid from view, and focused on sharing poetry at the continuation high school and primary school where I was working. Whatever light I could summon, I shone on the children; the light they shared with me kept me going.

Step by step for a couple more years before I began feeling better. I was slow to trust the returning tendrils of hope, but eventually opened the box I'd hidden and read all I'd written. The material didn't work, it was easy to see that, but I knew—yes—this is what I wanted to do, write the book Elmo had assigned more than six years before.

I'd always loved first person narratives—Sylvia Ashton-Warner's *Teacher*, Frank Conroy's *Stop-Time*, Anne Moody's *Coming of Age in Mississippi*—and memoir was the big publishing craze in 1996. I checked out volume after volume from the library. I read for enjoyment, of course, but also to study the form. I paid primary attention to what made me either warm to, or turn away from, a book. I tended to be bored with psychological cause-and-effect or a storyteller who felt sorry for herself. Despite that popular "show, don't tell" dictum, I liked narration, wanted a voice I could hear, and was most interested in a story larger than one individual life. I wanted observations that came through both *eye* and *I*.

Although I'd never been to any, I decided to apply for time at artist colonies. Free room and board and no task other than writing sounded like heaven. I figured if gave up my apartment, I'd need money only for storage, health care, plane fare to the colonies, postage, and a few phone calls. A figure certainly greater than zero, but not by an enormous amount. I received two acceptances and set off for almost four months, first to the Anderson Center in Red Wing, Minnesota, and then to Hedgebrook on Puget Sound.

Elmo—ally, critic, and teacher—was my biggest concern. Elmo was most often both righteous and right. Could I write reckless if I knew Elmo would read what I wrote? And yet who better than Elmo, the one who gave the assignment, to help me strengthen my book? I knew Elmo would hold me to the hard task I set for myself: to write from my most honest heart. I asked Elmo if he would be willing to give me editorial feedback. "You've got that coming," he wrote right back.

My sister and her family live in St. Paul and they drove me to Red Wing. As Emma, my then ten-year-old niece, noted it was as though I was going off to camp: the family would leave me on my own to make friends with strangers. The stranger I became closest to was Nancy Lord, at Anderson Center to finish her wonderful memoir, *Fishcamp*. In our evening talks I told Nancy that one of the challenges I faced, when I began writing my book all those years before, was that I wasn't sure how much of myself to put in the telling. I had felt that even though Elmo had assigned me to write my own experience, I should focus on my students.

Nancy responded by showing me a quote she had copied from a lecture by memoirist Patricia Hampl about how Whitman wrote "not *about* the self, but about *using* the self—as lens, as filter, as tool." This was the notion of self I had responded to so positively during my own memoir reading. Hampl went on in Nancy's quote: this self "is the right tool for the job which is the task of rendering the world." The task of rendering the complex world I'd been part of for four years is what I hoped to do. Nancy and the Hampl quote gave me courage.

Everything at the Anderson Center gave me courage: writing all day in my room as others worked in theirs, mealtime conversation, the Cannon River to explore on early morning bike rides and late afternoon walks. I wrote one hundred pages of a first draft as the colors outside my window changed from summer green to early fall yellows and reds.

Then I flew to Seattle. I stood at the door to my cabin the morning I arrived at Hedgebrook nearly stunned, filled—overflowing, really—with gratitude as I looked downhill toward Puget Sound. I couldn't believe I'd actually been given the gift of ten weeks to write in this gorgeous setting. Six women writers each had her own handcrafted cabin. Lunch was brought to us in baskets and we looked out at the Sound as we sat around the dinner table each evening. Many days, walking from my cabin to the main house, I could see Seattle to the southeast or the Olympics to the southwest.

My cabin was wood, glass, and woven blankets. I slept in a big bed in the loft, covered with quilts, listening to songbirds and owls. My typewriter sat on a huge desk and, for hours and hours each day, I settled into the writing. I'd given up my apartment, put my few things in storage, and so there was no home to miss; my Hedgebrook cabin and the book I was writing were home, which allowed me to go very deep as I wrote. I arrived at Hedgebrook during the sunny days of October and left after a light December snow. During those two and one half months, I finished a penultimate draft of the book.

Even now I find it hard to express the enormity of the gift. I did not have to shop, cook, clean, drive a car, or pay bills. No need even to arrange to see friends, because everyone at Hedgebrook showed up each night for dinner at the main house. My one task was to do what I most wanted to do: write the best I was able and bring all of myself to the work. The cabin—this is how it felt—became a container for the book I had been carrying since Elmo first gave me the assignment. I could put the book down, let the space around me hold the project, and simply write word by word.

I was forty-nine years old that fall and I'd been writing since the days of Miss Grimshaw. Like most artists, I'd had to say no to a great deal of life to have time to write. My poems were most often published, but received no big worldly welcome. Which was fine, the fate of most who've spent a life making art. But now I'd received this immeasurable gift. As far as I knew, there were no colonies for ditch diggers or school nurses. There were certainly none for my prison students, who wrote longhand in their cells assaulted by the sounds and smells of the cell block. I didn't know whether artists alone deserved a gift such as Hedgebrook, but recognized that no matter who deserved what, my task was to honor what I'd been given by taking it in.

While I settled into the lap of this gift, making the best use of it that I possibly could, others around me were doing the same. Hedgebrook wasn't 27 Rue de Fleurs or Cedar Tavern; the women in the other cabins weren't country neighbors as Kate had been; together we didn't form the group my students and I had at San Quentin. This was a new experience of community. Twelve or fifteen women came and went during my weeks at Hedgebrook. Most were like me, Kate, Lynnelle, and so many others: not famous but committed to making art.

Once I had drafts of chapters, I sent them to Elmo. His responses were clear, sharp, and smart, as I'd known they would be. He understood that my hope was to be, as he put it, "that passionate witness Neruda wrote about." Still he demanded, as he had during the four years I'd taught at San Quentin, that I recognize and acknowledge what I didn't—and, as an outsider, couldn't—know or understand. He defined for me even words I thought simple—lifer, murder—and explained the convict code and the nuance between shank and flat, piece, *keisu* and *fillero*. He wrote about prison: "Hatred like hands in the way it held me sometimes." Elmo always found the place in my writing where I hadn't gone far enough or been completely honest. Even when his suggested edits were not ones I used, his unerring nose for evasion and his insistence that I get prison right, made him the best editor I could possibly have worked with.

Of course Elmo was also a primary character in the story, and, when I read from the manuscript to other writers at Hedgebrook, Lisa Schlesinger said, "Oh, he's the one the reader is going to fall in love with!" I knew this assessment would please Elmo, especially as he'd been worried—since he had "instructed" me so forcefully at Quentin—that he would come off in my book as some hot-headed heavy. I sent him Lisa's words in my very next letter.

Love. Such a loaded word when the subject is a woman working in a men's prison. I hadn't fallen in love with any of my students, hadn't sneaked into a broom closet for a quickie, hadn't quit my job to marry a man in blue, or secretly pined and sighed over one when alone by myself. Yet love was at the heart of my years at San Quentin and was, in so many ways, the subject of the book I was writing.

Love was sharing big sis soul talk with Spoon, witnessing Coties's concern for his children, listening to Smokey quietly speak of the death of his son's mother, observing Elmo do his best to make comfortable every guest artist visiting our class, reading about Chris's death in that cell fight. Love was my own heart and spirit expanding.

When I read my first chapter to the women at Hedgebrook, the word love appeared on nearly page one. Again Lisa spoke. She said love was too easy a word at the start; my book had to earn love, had to take the reader through my experience at Quentin so that by the end, when the word love appeared, it contained enough force to pop the reader's heart open. Lisa's words gave me the secret, the center, the thread to weave through every page of my book.

Whether a reader did, or didn't, fall in love with Elmo, I was certainly growing closer to him myself. Early on, Spoon and I had found a way of knowing each other through poetry, and Spoon continued to send me support and "write reckless" encouragement as I worked on the book. Elmo demanded a more straightforward exchange and now that I was free of prison restrictions, I was happy for the sharing our correspondence began.

In one letter, Elmo mentioned Herbert Marcuse's *One-Dimensional Man*—a book that had been must-reading for my generation in college. Elmo let me know that he himself wasn't one dimensional, never had been, and that for him, "knowing someone, really knowing someone and having someone know you, has to be all about being seen in ones entirety, warts and all, having the courage to be that honest within yourself and with others."

I sat in the alcove of my Hedgebrook cabin, holding the nine double-sided pages of Elmo's letter as I stared out the window, wondering. You mean being seen and knowing each other is what Elmo had wanted back when I thought he was angry with me or being judgmental? What I'd taken in as criticism had really been intended as an invitation?

The sky was blue outside the glass and my gaze loose as I imagined what it might feel like to be Elmo—strong, self-confident, sure—with one's gifts perceived as a problem in the world of prison. I'd always known that Spoon's spirit needed the natural world—birds, a warm breeze, desert sands—and that he searched for any slight green sprouting inside prison walls. Now I saw how deeply Elmo's spirit needed complex human relationships and how that need was probably even harder to come by than flowers or wild cats when locked behind bars.

My hope, during the years I spent at San Quentin, had been to hold up those mirrors; in that world of such darkness, I wanted to reflect light. Since I didn't really know how to do that, I just threw myself into the intention. I couldn't tell if my efforts were useful at all, so it made me very happy when Elmo wrote me: "I always smiled when you pulled up to my bars, because you were always the open window through which my beleaguered heart and soul could feel a moment of fresh air and some sunshine." Instead of silencing me, as I had feared, Elmo's letters encouraged me to dig deeper, to write better, to proceed despite doubt. Instead of a critic, I found a friend.

One night, after I returned from Hedgebrook, Elmo called from Mule Creek where he was then housed. I'd been struggling to find the right title for my book and Elmo called to offer the title of one of his own poems: "Disguised as a Poem." I was incredibly moved, both at the generosity of Elmo's gift, and at how well Elmo's phrase fit my book.

I sent *Disguised as a Poem: My Years Teaching Poetry at San Quentin* off to an agent. Ten days later, on a Sunday afternoon, she called to tell me she loved my book and thought it the best new work she'd read in years. She put her husband on the phone, as he'd read and loved *Disguised* as well. I'd just turned fifty and, for the first time in my life, I felt seen in a way I had assumed I never would be. The agent—a big New York agent—was sure she'd sell my book in a flash.

But she didn't. She didn't sell it at all.

I was tempted to put my manuscript back in the box in which I'd hid it for years, but knew I owed better to the men whose humanity I wanted the world to see. I owed my family and friends, too, colony colleagues, and the colonies themselves, all of whom had given me so much support. So I vowed to be a bulldog, but now for my own work. The effort took me two years, but in October 1999 I got a call from Northeastern University Press, and *Disguised* was published the following fall.

14

Annotation

I HAD HOPED to get a letter from Saga in Sweden telling me she was pregnant. We tried on our final overnight visit to make a baby, but it didn't happen. About a year after she was back home in Sweden, Saga wrote and told me she'd had a baby by a jazz player. I was happy for her, but sad we didn't create the baby we had longed for.

I dived deeper into playwriting to channel the heavy blows life had been giving my heart and spirit. I read somewhere that to write your best you must read the best, so I read William Stafford, Lucile Clifton, Pablo Neruda, Mary Oliver, Maya Angelou, Shakespeare, Langston Hughes, Ibsen, August Wilson, Strindberg, Genet, Beckett, Chekov, Dickens, Oscar Wilde, James Baldwin, Richard Wright, E.B. White, W.E.B. Dubois, and many others. Whatever form I chose to work in, for that time, that's what I read and studied.

I decided not to write Judith unless and until I was transferred away from Folsom. A mutual friend of ours, poet Kate Dougherty, became my second writing mentor through the mail. Kate had known Judith for years and had even come to our poetry class to teach about making books. Kate worked with me on my first piece of fiction, giving me wisdom on paragraph and sentence structure, particularly on my use of sentence fragments. Kate constantly reminded me about verb tense. She educated me about the difference between active and passive verbs and about the power of strong nouns.

My study of great literature led me to the C-Yard library where I met and befriended a tall, white prisoner named Pat Nolan. I had been sent to C-Yard a few months after the big riot on B-Yard. Pat worked at the C-Yard library and I was there checking out prose and poetry. Pat and I talked and discovered that we were both studying the classics. I ran down my Arts-in-Corrections and prison history to him. Pat ran down his story. He had come from Canada to be an American white racist gangster. He found out the gangster life did not suit, nor live up to, his rebel expectations. While in the hole, Pat discovered he was a poet.

I shared a lot of my poetry with Pat and he shared his work with me. Anytime a new batch of literature came to the library, Pat made sure I had first choice. He and I boldly walked the yard, which was racially segregated, and spoke about poetry and how it moved us and opened up both of our lives.

I told Pat that, after the way I was treated in Arts-in-Corrections at San Quentin after the success of *Waiting for Godot*, I could not be a part of that program again. Right after the play was done, Arts-in-Corrections did nothing to stop my transfer to Old Folsom. Yet when Arts-in-Corrections finally made it to New Folsom and brought in a creative writing program, Pat wanted me to join with him in founding the class.

I said, "No way!" But brother Pat's persistence on something he wanted or believed in has become legendary. He convinced me to join him in the writing class run by Dianna Henning.

Pat and I had begun to study poetic scansion, meter, form, and structure on our own. I had not studied how to build a poem formally before. Judith had taught me by inspiration and imagination coming from the heart and soul. Dianna ran her class in a more formal manner. She gave out lines for the class and a booklet that defined and gave examples of all the terms and inner workings of a poem. I studied those poetic terms and definitions as I had the regular dictionary when at the beginning of my journey in prison.

Dianna introduced me to doing annotations on poems. I went poem- and annotation-crazy. I turned in so much writing, Dianna asked me to slow down. She told me that she could only accept two annotations or poems each week. We turned in material one week and Dianna gave it back with comments and suggestions the following week.

Although even prison officials told me I should never have been sent to Folsom, it took two years for them to transfer me. A week or two after I was moved from New Folsom, Judith came to Dianna's class as a guest artist.

In 1991, I was transferred to Donovan, the prison near San Diego. I went to the Board of Prison Terms just before leaving New Folsom and that was an unexpected high note. The deputy commissioner of the Board told me that I did not have enough time in on my crime for him to recommend a pardon or clemency; he said the political atmosphere was not ripe at the state house. But he told me that I would appear before the Board again in three years. He had read in my file that I was a published writer and he spoke about Oscar Wilde and other writers. He suggested that I write my way out of prison.

His words sounded good because I knew I would continue to write and act if the opportunity arose. I wondered: How does one write his way out of prison? Who decides if a text is good enough to give a prisoner a second chance in the free world? Is it the number of books written, the number of articles, essays, and poems published, the number of awards won? I like to think it's how many hearts and souls are touched in honest and deep ways. The Board noted that I would enhance any prison I was housed in.

Donovan was way more open than Folsom. It did not have any trees, but mud swallows were there. I watched the birds paste their mud hotels on the sides of buildings. There were miles-long floating caravans of Monarch butterflies flying down the coast of California to Mexico each year and this event lasted all day. There was night yard and a huge track to walk.

I had heard about another prison in central California called California Men's Colony, which was supposed to have better programming than Donovan. Also, and most important to me, at CMC-East I could get a single-man cell. I asked the counselor about a transfer to CMC-East. He instantly agreed and received approval from the warden and from Sacramento where they created a chrono—a behavior report—which stated that, despite my life without possibility of parole sentence, I should be treated like any level-three prisoner and that no further Department of Review Board order from Sacramento would be required to transfer me to any level three prison. I was set. I would never have to go back up to a higher-level prison again unless I broke a prison rule, committed another crime, went insane, or something like that.

I arrived at CMC-East in the middle of summer and was amazed by all the plants, flowers, and vegetable gardens. There were palm trees, oak trees, evergreen trees, and bushes. There were some trees as tall as light poles and others with hanging moss. There were thick trees that grew like vines, with fat purple flowers. I had never seen trees that blossom like flowers. We did not have those in the desert. There were dense bushes against walls and fences and tall sunflowers in corners, each one packed with sunflower seeds. The vegetable and flower gardens were around every corner.

We were given keys to our cell rooms, as opposed to being slammed into barred cages. The library was huge and there were education classes on each of the four quads plus in the prison plaza—two corridors full of academic and vocational classrooms.

There was a wooden bench beside the chow hall, under a big shade tree on C-Yard, from which I could look out on a majestic mountain full of greenery. Railroad tracks curled around the mountain and long trains circled the mountain as they pulled up and over it. Sometimes I could see the beginning, middle, and end of the same train.

There were little wooden fences around gardens. Hawks of different sizes caught sparrows and black birds; sparrows and black birds caught insects. I eventually built up such a splendid rapport with some sparrows and black birds that they followed me all over the prison and even flew into the classroom where I was. Whenever I whistled, they flew over fences, buildings, and down from roofs and rafters.

The cell rooms had fat, barless, windows where I saw deer, crows, turkey vultures, and red-tailed hawks. Possums lived under the business education trailer, raised their young, and eventually raided my vegetable and flower gardens. We could put sodas in our cell windows to keep them cold.

Just before dawn, I watched crows and seagulls joust in the sky for ownership. There were tennis courts and walking paths on each yard. You could sit, lie down, or sleep on the grass. The red-breasted finches made their nests and raised their young in hanging houseplants right next to the teacher's desk. Prisoners ran around with pet snakes and lizards.

I was told by an education counselor that CMC-East was a transitional prison—that those housed there were on their way to the streets—and that I had to find my own job in the prison. I believed this. I believed I was on my way out. I would stop off in Barstow to visit the graves of my mother, aunt, and other family members, then I would be off to Sweden and then to Paris to visit Samuel Beckett's grave.

I took my publishing history to a cool teacher and she instantly hired me as a teacher's aide. I helped students read and write. The teacher allowed me to develop and direct short plays in the library. My students performed before other classes as well. It was refreshing to be on stage, even doing small time directing, keeping alive and passing on what I had learned from Jan, Bill Irwin, Alice Smith, and Samuel Beckett.

My teacher took me with her to teachers' meetings where I gave poetry readings. I also went to other classes to give readings. A college program was held at the prison at night, and when they found out I was a published writer, I gave poetry readings there, too, receiving college credit in my communications class.

A Cal Poly professor from the Black History department at the college contacted CMC-East's education department and asked if she could come inside the prison and videotape me giving a poetry reading. She wanted to use my work in her department, which would pay for the entire process. The Education department at the prison said no. I could not figure out why. Who or what would the film hurt? It reminded me of the negative imaginative spin put on the Point Arena School letter exchange that would have allowed me to write the teachers and students in their classrooms. This was that "setting up a prisoner as hero" bullshit again.

I went to the education office and asked the college counselor—she was the one who had introduced my work to Cal Poly—why the video was not allowed. She told me it was not her call. So I waited for the head administrator of the college program at CMC-East.

"You speak of free thinkers in college and teach us to think for ourselves. You cannot make me believe my doing a poetry reading for Cal Poly is negative."

"You don't understand."

I had also written an essay wondering how Chapman College could be a true program when it denied freedom of speech and positive expression. I had turned the essay into my college communications class. The professor felt it was her duty to show the essay to her boss.

"Another thing, Mr. Jackson," the administrator pulled out my essay. "How could you write this?"

"How could you tell me that doing a poetry reading is negative?"

"If you don't think our college program is real, you don't have to attend."

"Writing an essay is my freedom of speech. Cal Poly asked to film me and poetry readings are part of most college programs. All my essay explores is how you could twist something positive into something negative and still call your program higher education."

"If you keep writing essays like this, we can take you out of our program."

The administrator took a couple of deep breaths, calmed down, and retracted her threat. The video was never made.

Three years passed and I asked about going back to the Board of Prison Terms. The counselor sent a notice back in the mail that all Board hearings for life without prisoners had been postponed until further notice.

Five more years passed and college programs and Pell grants ceased for all prisoners. Weights were taken away from the yard. An associate warden from up north came to CMC-East. They called him a troubleshooter. There had been no trouble at CMC-East. In fact, an old school lieutenant had told a couple of us prisoners that if the entire yard was full of lifers, he could run the yard by himself.

The troubleshooter associate warden proceeded to dismantle CMC-East. He raised the custody level of all the lifers and moved us all to inside cells overlooking the prison yard. He no longer allowed lifers to visit on the outside patio of the visiting room. He chopped down all the trees and bushes, and pulled up the flower and vegetable gardens. The birds began to disappear. The associate warden said he did not want any plant life taller than grass. Some of the trees had been there for decades, perhaps millennia. The associate warden decided he did not want any life withouts at CMC-East, and to justify this, he said it was because there were no electric fences. I had been at CMC-East for eight years, had established a good program there, and had met some inspiring local people.

Years had passed since my love with Saga and I decided to reach out. A local paper printed personal ads from prisoners and free people and I read this ad: "Green-eyed blonde, 30, been stuck in marriage of convenience. Want to rediscover passion with a man who smells good, drives fast, and has a soul. I love books, philosophy, the ocean, and '70s rock."

I wrote her and sent an article containing my poems. We exchanged a few letters, and in no time, Briana came to visit. She had on a light green blouse, a white skirt that hovered just above her smooth knees, and pearl white one-strapped sandals that highlighted her toes. I could not take my eyes off them, except to look into Briana's eyes. Our conversations were vast. We spoke on almost every subject. We both admired Ralph Waldo Emerson's essays and other writings. I recited Shakespeare and some of my poems to Briana on visits.

Briana looked like a thick Sharon Stone. She told me doctors, lawyers, and other big-shot men had wooed her with dinner and jewelry. She had gone out with a few. But in the end, she chose me, a poet in prison.

Briana brought both her children, Nancy and Sid, to visit. They both liked and loved me instantly. Nancy knew her mom had become my best friend. Nancy was about four or five at the time. I told her that she was my little best friend and she said, "I know." I wrote a short fairy tale for her called *Nancy's Garden*. The whole family loved it. I promised Nancy that it would be published someday.

Briana was every bit as beautiful as her ad had boasted. She turned heads in the visiting room. She was a brilliant writer of screenplays, nonfiction, new-age books, and articles. She gave sage advice and edits of my stage plays and fiction. She knew how to bring characters, drama, and conflicts to life with truth and eloquence. We were both married to other people. Briana put in for her divorce and, after she contacted Saga in Sweden, she put in for my divorce with Saga's blessings.

Briana was smart and gifted, not only as a writer, mother, and editor, but she also knew how to organize and get things done. She wrote a gripping article about visiting at CMC-East, describing how visitors were mistreated and disrespected. Prison staff left visitors to stand in long lines outside when it was cold and rainy, even though there was a large unused waiting room where people could step out of the bad weather. The article was published in a local paper that many people in the San Luis Obispo area read. Briana, who lived about twenty minutes from the prison, had mailed the article to me, yet, two weeks later, I had not received my copy.

The mailroom and visiting room were both under the control of the same lieutenant. Briana and I were sitting in the visiting room enjoying our visit when this redheaded lieutenant brought Briana's letter with the enclosed article to me. He asked us to come over to a secluded section of the visiting room.

"I don't appreciate this article putting down my visiting officers!"

157

I looked at Briana and said, "I see what happened to my copy."

The lieutenant continued, "If you keep writing this shit, don't expect to get any family visits."

"Briana, baby, you can write whatever you want."

I told the lieutenant, "What she wrote must be true, or you would not be delivering mail personally on someone's visit."

We went back to our visit. I could not believe what had happened. It showed how powerful Briana's words were. I was so proud of her. The lieutenant's threats and withholding of the mail were wrong and illegal and we could have sued. But Briana really wanted family visits, so we decided to keep our pens away from certain topics, at least for a while.

On our next visit, the lieutenant came over and apologized. Although another time, he pulled Briana over before she came inside to visit and told her why I was in prison, hoping to discourage her from marrying me. His tactic did not work. I had told Briana from the start why I was in prison. We went on with our wedding plans.

Briana had had a rough upbringing, which was one of the reasons she could write so powerfully, deep, and real. She was raised by a single mom who was a small-time actress and a big-time partier. The mom often brought the parties home, having sex with strange men who roamed the house and stayed over all night. Briana and her two sisters had to raise themselves.

Briana and I did cancel our wedding, though. Not because of any threats, but because the state took away family overnight visits.

Briana was a sexy leopard with lemon-colored toes. I loved reading to her on visits. She was very amorous and sexual. We always sat as close as possible, trying to inhale each other's breath and heartbeats. She could have sweet earthquakes just sitting together, hand in hand.

Briana could not go long without having sex. I could not blame her. What a terrible torture to put someone through. If you truly love someone, you don't want them to suffer and be in prison along with you. Even though it hurt like a vise grip, I understood. We remained friends and felt love all the moments we were together, but the visits and contact went from a lot, to some, to a little, and then to none.

Every year or so, Briana contacted me and told me she had been following me on my website. The last time Briana and I spoke, she told me she had won a nationwide screenplay-writing contest. She won a cash award of $20,000 and a contract with Warner Brothers Studio, which had sponsored the contest.

Now Briana writes crime dramas for a major network and for TV specials. I don't hear from her anymore, and I hope the reason is not that she's made it. But even if it is, I am proud of her and still believe in her and in her brilliant kids who have excelled in high school and college. I sometimes wonder if they remember me.

After Briana and I moved on, I got involved with a food sale where the men inside bought food and donated money to a youth program for abused teenagers. We also decided to post a card to the shelter to show our support and encouragement of the young people. A few months later, I was contacted by a nineteen-year-old girl who told me she had been one of the young women at the shelter. Penny had seen my name in some paper and she remembered me from the card. She said she took seeing my name as a sign to write me. After we exchanged a few letters, Penny wanted to come visit, so she told her Mom, Annie, about me. Annie wrote, and then came to visit me first, to make sure I was cool before her daughter came to visit. Annie and I became friends.

I was seeing another woman at the time and was not looking for anything serious. I did not want to put another woman through the agony—the torture—of doing prison time. Annie thought she could handle the prison beast, this monster that eats galaxies, disrupts and destroys lives on so many unseen and unthought-of levels. Prison could make death seem only unpleasant in comparison. Still, the longing for a hug and kiss, even a brief hug and kiss—a touch—can be magical to a prisoner and seem to last forever.

Annie thought of us as boyfriend and girlfriend and I did not object. I did not push her away or say we could only be friends. When other visitors, officers, and prisoners told Annie another woman also visited me, she cried.

I asked, "What do you want to do, get married?"

She said yes so fast I could not figure out a way to take it back, though I did remind her, "There are no more family visits."

"I can handle it."

"Just go without making love or having sex?"

"Yes! I've done that before. There are other ways of doing things. It won't take too long to get you out of prison." Annie really believed she could get me out in no time.

I was still not over Briana. Annie was more in love with me than I with her. Still, we got married at the end of summer.

We had visits at CMC-East for about three and one-half years, never consummating our marriage. The strain and pain of the ordeal was crazy. Annie made it seem like the lack of sex did not matter, that we could let go and live off the thoughts, vibes, and feelings of sex and be happy with what we had. She felt we could dream of making love on our own—me in the cell and her in a big waterbed at home. Annie was a splendid friend and woman, another artist, a painter like Saga. She was always there and walked the earth in her own way. My first mind had told me not to get married again in prison unless family visits came back. But I did get married and family visits for lifers are—to this day—still forbidden.

After the troubleshooter associate warden pushed to get life withouts out of his prison, I was transferred to Lancaster prison in Los Angeles County. Annie lived over three hundred miles away and visits were very expensive, so they became once or twice a month.

There was only one Arts-in-Corrections class on my yard at Lancaster. The class was on screenwriting, and it was taught by a writer from Hollywood. He taught us the basics of creating screenplays. We all worked on one screenplay together for practice. Each student was assigned two characters to flesh out in scenes using a common theme. The book we used was *The Complete Screenwriter's Bible*.

I read, pondered, and studied the book from cover to cover. I created my own screenplay as I learned. Our instructor was asked to go to Hawaii to write a screenplay on surfing. He could not turn down a sun-filled job on an island. He never showed up at Lancaster again. I was sad about that, but his job was screenwriting and teaching in prison was a hobby. I kept *The Complete Screenwriter's Bible*.

There was no way to get out of the sun at Lancaster. There were ravens at this desert prison, and if you left your lunch on a table, ravens would unwrap, eat, or carry it away in no time. I sometimes gave them my lunch. I was at Lancaster for about two years and then I was transferred to Pleasant Valley State Prison.

There were no trees at Pleasant Valley, but there were flowers, bushes, and roses against the inside perimeter fence. There was a little fishpond with boulders, roses, other plants, and with flowers around it. I had a cool clerk's job in Special Purchase helping prisoners order appliances, fans, TVs, radios, musical instruments, clothes, and shoes.

When the yard was cleared at noon for lunch, I stayed out at the fish pond and watched the fish. Also the hummingbirds did not mind my looking at them from only a foot away as they sipped the flowers that surrounded the pond.

At night I sat on a big boulder beside the pond and watched the sky. Every night a white owl flew by at the same hour. Bats feasted on fat moths and other insects caught in the prison lights. When the owl came by, it was my sign that it was almost time for yard recall.

There were wild cats roaming the prison, and each group had its own area right next to the chow halls on all four yards. The alpha female cat on A-Yard, where I was housed, often came up to me and rubbed against my leg. Sometimes she brought her kittens. I shared milk and sardines with them.

I helped found the only Arts-in-Corrections class there, the Pleasant Valley State Prison Acting Troupe, which was run by free actor, director, and writer, Dean Brooks, who had played in the "Incredible Hulk" series on TV many years before. Dean had us do improv. He was allowed to video-tape some scenes, but I was told he was only allowed one cartridge, so he repeatedly recorded over what came before.

Dean was white and totally fascinated by George Washington Carver and Booker T. Washington. He felt their history had never been fully told, appreciated, or explored, so he wrote a play based on the historical meetings of Carver, W.E.B. Dubois, Washington, and a couple of others. He even had a song in the script written by Stevie Wonder, who believed in Dean's cause. I played Booker T. Washington in the scenes we rehearsed. We also performed Dickens' *A Christmas Carol* in the prison chapel in two performances of short scenes. I played the narrator and Marley, the ghost. We received great response from the audience.

My wife, Annie, had moved from near CMC-East to Coalinga, minutes away from Pleasant Valley, so I received visits every week. This visiting room had the best food—complete homemade dinners from Fresno—at reasonable prices, especially when compared to the other prisons where I had been.

I was Special Purchase clerk for almost four years, but then the administration decided it did not want a prisoner to be at one job for more than two years. I was laid off without notice and assigned to the kitchen on a split shift as a line server. I went to work from 4:00 to 8:00 AM and then from 3:30 to 7:00 PM. The cool thing about working in the chow hall was that I got to know and feed the cats more often. I watched them growl, grow, mate, and hunt. The alpha female was the leader, of course, and the bravest of her clan. She came up to get the sardines, meat, and milk as if she owned the ground she walked on. The kittens watched her, turning their little heads, soaking in all the lessons.

Sometimes, after I completed my tasks, I assisted the linebackers who cleaned and cleared the chow line. Once, after we'd cleared the line, some crazy workers filled a big trash can with oatmeal and carted it outside on the dock to the big green slop dumpsters. The workers were too weak to lift it. Besides, it was not wise to fill a big barrel up with oatmeal. It must have weighed about 300 or 400 pounds. The dumpsters stood about four feet high. The prisoners who had created the mess looked on dumbfounded.

I had taken some basic trash out to the bins. When the correctional officer in charge saw me he said, "Jackson, come help dump this trash."

I walked over and saw the big trash can full of oatmeal, "That is not going to happen."

According to most custody staff, the correctional officer was always right, even when wrong. "Are you refusing to work?" the officer asked.

"No."

"Then lift the can."

"That is not going to happen."

"Are you refusing a direct order?"

"No. But if you ordered me to jump off the tier, I wouldn't do that either."

The officer turned red and the other prisoners looked on in disbelief. The cook—who was a free man—came over, picked up on the dilemma, and said in a full voice to everyone, "That is too much weight. Hell, I would not lift it either."

The officer still insisted I help lift the crap. When I just stared at him, he told me to leave his chow hall and that I would get a write-up for disobeying a direct order.

I went to the sergeant's office and described the problem. He and I went back to the chow hall. The trash can full of oatmeal was still in the same spot. The sergeant spoke with the free cook and the officer inside the office. The sergeant told the officer he could not write me up. He told him to make the idiots who dumped all the oatmeal break the mess up.

I was sent to my cell, where I found a letter from Jan. Jan Jonson, my Swedish brother from *Godot* days, wrote that he had developed a stage show about Samuel Beckett and the performances by Kumla and San Quentin prisoners. He said he told my story and also read some of my poetry during the performance. He wrote that he sat on a chair between poster-sized photos of Samuel Beckett and me and began his show by reading my poems "No Beauty in Cell Bars," "Beauty in Cell Bars," and "Chair," which I'd written for Samuel Beckett. Jan wrote that his performance was called *Moments of Reality*. Jan traveled all over Europe for fifteen years doing this show. Others have since written and told me that he kept the audience—young people and old people—spellbound for nearly six hours.

During one of Jan's performances in Sweden, a composer, conductor, musician, and filmmaker, Michel Wenzer, sat in the audience. Michel was so blown away by Jan's performance, and by his connection to me and my story, that he wrote me. After Michel contacted me, we became friends and brothers. Michel, along with a well-known Swedish photographer, Albin Biblom, came to Pleasant Valley State Prison to visit. They had come to the USA to do a short documentary film on me and my poetry. They went to Barstow to film where I grew up and they spoke with some of my family. *Three Poems by Spoon Jackson* turned out beautifully—pictures blended with poems. The short film has traveled the world, playing in film festivals and winning a few awards.

During one visit, Michel, Albin, and I took some pictures in the visiting room. For one of them, we held up the peace sign. The visiting room sergeant said we could not keep the photos because no gang signs were allowed. I held up the peace sign and asked, "What gang is this? The peace gang?"

"Still, you cannot do hand gestures in photos."

My Swedish brothers and I smiled, laughed, and decided to start the Peace Gang to promote peace, love, peoplehood, forgiveness, and harmony with Mother Earth.

After four years at Pleasant Valley, the administration decided to change the prison to protective custody/sensitive needs, starting with A-Yard, where I was housed. The captain had permission to send almost everyone from

A-Yard to Old Folsom. The only yard that would not be sensitive needs would be B-Yard. My wife, Annie, was only ten minutes away from the prison, so when the captain and his classification committee tried to rubber-stamp me back to Old Folsom, I asked why I could not go to B-Yard. The captain's face seemed to be plotting something. He said, "Sure. B-Yard it is."

B-Yard seemed to be cool. I got to meet up and mingle again with Happy and Twin, two of the old cast members from *Waiting for Godot* days. But then the counselor summoned me to her office and said, "You are placed out of your custody level."

"What are you talking about? I have been here at Pleasant Valley on A-Yard for over four years."

"You are supposed to be at a level four."

Level four is the highest security level prison. I said, "I am supposed to be where I am."

The counselor was black, the two sergeants were black, the lieutenant was black, and the captain was black. I repeated that I had been on A-Yard for over four years. The counselor said someone hadn't been doing his job. I now knew why the white captain on A-Yard hadn't fought my protest against being sent to Old Folsom. He knew I would regret my request to stay at Pleasant Valley.

I had heard crazy stories about the female black captain on B-Yard. I heard she ran out in the middle of the yard by herself during a full-scale race riot, waving her hands, and jumping up and down like a maniac. She ordered all combatants to get on the ground. I also heard that, even though a prisoner had served his time in the hole, when she sat on the release committee the black captain wanted him to stay longer. Even some guards smiled when they spoke of her unbending ways, how she looked for confrontation when there was none, and in such a case she made up some conflict.

I like to check out things for myself and figured, even if the captain was crazy, I would give her fifty feet and would have no reason to deal with her except once a year during my annual review. If I did deal with her, I would dazzle her with my clean, progressive, positive record.

The black counselor took me before the classification committee on B-Yard. On the panel sat the black captain, lieutenant, and sergeant. There were also a white counselor and white representatives of the education and medical departments. I had never met the captain before, yet she acted as though I had kicked her dog or spat on her. She told the sergeant and an officer to stand behind me. I could not believe the drama. Even when I had been at higher level prisons, such devotion to security had not been needed. The white folks on the panel seemed puzzled, considering my record, about why the captain was so harsh.

"I cannot have someone on my yard serving life without," said the captain.

Before I could speak, the black counselor jumped in. "Inmate Jackson was not happy when I advised him he was out of placement here."

"I've been at level three ... "

I was interrupted by the captain. "You will be transferred to a level four prison."

It was as if I did not exist. The captain looked at the other counselor and said, "We can transfer him to Salinas Valley level four as soon as possible. I want him out of here."

She told the sergeant, after the hearing, "Make sure you measure his dreads, and if they are over three inches, write him up."

The captain was still speaking as I was escorted out of classification. The sergeant never did measure my hair, which was about an inch long at the time. I felt empty, not having a voice at the committee. It was all absurd, but I knew I was on my way out of Pleasant Valley State Prison.

I could not figure out why all the black administrators piled on top of me as if we were playing tackle football. The black female officer at the desk of B-Yard visiting always gave my wife, Annie—who was white—a hard time. She would delay her from going to and from restroom breaks and would go out of her way to put people in front of my wife when she came to and from visiting.

I could not figure out the benefit gained by the black administration in transferring me. Was it because I had a white wife? Was it because of my life sentence? Perhaps they did not want to seem soft on someone of their own color.

I have noticed, among a lot of black correctional officers, some go out of their way to be stricter and harsher on black prisoners in the hopes of showing their white counterparts that they are not displaying favoritism. I even overheard the black prison chaplain on B-Yard telling some officers that he was not one of them, meaning the prisoners. The prison population on B-Yard knew that chaplain's feelings, and so on Sundays, instead of going into the chapel for services, prisoners held church on the yard—black, brown, and white prisoners in one big circle.

I wondered what evil powers moved the black captain and her crew to want me back up to a higher level prison when my in-custody behavior had been one of steady progress and atonement. I knew there must be some blessing, some realness to be reaped, from such an unwarranted act. I had not threatened any officers, free staff, or other prisoners. Sure, I had castigated a few people verbally, but I had not put hands on anybody. I knew deep down that this transfer would close my marriage to Annie. She deserved better. I could not ask her to follow me and to keep putting her life and plans on hold. I wanted her to go on with her life and to have all the love and sex she wanted. I wanted Annie to have fun and enjoy the freedom of not doing time anymore. It had been seven years.

The black captain wanted me to go to Salinas Valley, one of the worst institutions in California. Salinas Valley State Prison often stayed on lockdown nine or ten months of the year.

15

Power or Prison

ELMO READ *Disguised as a Poem* chapter by chapter as I worked on the book; Spoon and Coties read the manuscript's penultimate version. I sent the material to everyone else mentioned in the text when I knew the book would be published. I asked each man whether he'd prefer I use his real name or a pseudonym, for permission to use his poems, and to see if he wanted a copy of the book when it appeared. The letters my former students wrote back had a consistent message, one that went something like this: "Thank you for showing us as human beings. I might have written about that time differently, but you presented your experience honestly from your point of view." Over the years, *Disguised* has received some nice reviews, as well as many kind letters and emails of praise. I'm thankful for every good word. But the notes from the men with whom I shared those four years are, of course, the ones that mean most.

The summer before the book came out, I attended a gathering of artists who also worked in prison. Buzz Alexander, professor at the University of Michigan and founder of the Prison Creative Arts Project (PCAP) there, assembled the group along with actor, writer, and composer Michael Keck. The long weekend was hosted by Blue Mountain Center in the Adirondacks. Buzz wrote: "We are a group of artists, activists, educators, and organizers who are opposed to the massive incarceration going on in our country. We are appalled and hurt by what we know, by the fact that we have well over a million of our citizens in federal and state prisons and many, many more in jails, juvenile detention centers, on probation and parole; by the fact that a dramatically disproportionate number of prisoners are African American, Latino, and poor people in general; by the fact that the prison-industrial complex is making immense profits off these prisoners; and by the real and devastating results we see in real lives. We are reminded of other times in other countries and in our own when citizens stood by while targeted economic, religious, and ethnic groups were criminalized, displaced, incarcerated, and executed in large numbers. We prefer not to be among the bystanders."

In our Arts-in-Corrections office at San Quentin, and at the annual statewide gatherings we held in the '80s, one frequent topic of conversation had been the challenge of doing work that was so intense and yet also hidden. Most prisons are in remote locations, and though voters and legislative bodies make frequent decisions about whom to lock up and for how long, few of these decision-makers have much actual experience with penal institutions or the people inside them. We—Arts-in-Corrections teaching artists and artist facilitators—*did* have actual experience.

Our friends and family were often interested in hearing our stories, but they had very little firsthand knowledge to help them imagine the reality behind what they heard. So talking to each other, in the office and at our annual conference, was a relief. For even if Jan Dove was artist facilitator at a women's prison and I worked with men, even though Beth Thielen created handmade books with women in Southern California and Lynnelle painted with men on death row, we had all experience working for months on a project only to have prison authorities, or a lockdown, or the transfer of a primary prisoner artist put an end to that effort. We'd all seen our students' reactions after receiving word of a parent's death, a child's illness, or a girlfriend's murder; we'd all watched as they made some kind of peace with being unable to be present for loved ones during a hard time; we'd all tried to give appropriate comfort. We'd all been asked to do something we were not allowed to do. We all knew the paintings and poems of people the world thought of as demons; we all knew our students as complex human beings.

The gathering at Blue Mountain provided a similar opportunity to share, not only the work we each did, but also the challenges and joys of that work. And to share, not only with Arts-in-Corrections colleagues in California prisons, but with people working through a variety of programs in a number of states. We spoke about our work, our experience, and our feelings. Each one of us was committed, not only to sharing art with people inside prison, but also to recognizing that what we witnessed as we did this work obliged us to speak to the larger world about what we saw.

As we talked at Blue Mountain, we felt the absence of those we knew who were locked up. We were frustrated and sad that these men and women, so much a part of our conversation, were not able to be with us. Years before, at San Quentin, Coties had written:

Say how ya doing
Outside world?
Do you remember me?
I'm that intricate part
Missing from the whole
The one y'all decided to forget…

We hadn't forgotten, but we definitely missed Coties and so many others. In fact, "missing" was one of our primary subjects. At some point in our three days together, we gathered into a circle and called out the names of those we recognized as part of our gathering though they were unable to be with us in person: Coties, Elmo, Spoon …

Disguised came out in September 2000, eleven years after Elmo had given me the assignment to write it, and my book described a world that no longer existed. In those eleven years, in California alone, the state's prison population had nearly tripled. Although there is a great deal of evidence that education and staying close with one's family are among the most positive predictors of making a successful life once released, college programs disappeared when Pell grants to prisoners were abolished in 1994, and family visits, such as those Spoon and Saga shared, had been banned for many, including most of my former students. Programming in general had diminished and Arts-in-Corrections itself had been dramatically cut.

Jim Rowland—the director of the California Department of Corrections when our warden okayed the San Quentin production of *Godot*—talked about rehabilitation this way. He said that some people in prison weren't ready to take a more positive route no matter what classes and programs were offered, while some were so ready to change their lives they didn't need any impetus. But, Rowland said, the majority was in the middle. These men and women needed a vast array of possibilities because

169

people are different, and some might be inspired by poetry and others by car repair. Rowland said that his job, therefore, was to offer a large and wide range of programming. I agreed with Rowland, but he didn't last long in his job and his vision had not prevailed.

By the time *Disguised* came out in 2000, most of my San Quentin students had served more than twenty years. Spoon—no matter that he'd awakened to his niche, as he called it, publishing poems and performing in *Godot*—was still locked up. Coties—the only man I met inside who said he had nothing to do with the crime for which he was convicted—was still inside. Elmo—who was present when his brother spontaneously shot and killed a man and whose seven-to-life sentence was meant, when given, to run about twelve years—was still inside. None of my students was what the world calls a "political prisoner," but many remained locked up because politicians had discovered that being tough on crime won elections. This discovery prompted legislators to add to the activities considered criminal and to increase the length of sentences and parole as well as the intensity of the public's fear. *Disguised* didn't offer political analysis, but I didn't want readers to forget this larger context of my students' lives.

So I met with a publicist for one hour's worth of advice. I would have the primary responsibility for putting my book out in the world, and I hoped for some tips that would help me. Nina began with a question that surprised me. "Which do you want most?" she asked. "To sell copies or to talk to the public about the issues?" I had assumed these goals were the same, or at least that their purposes overlapped. But the publicist said no, the two intentions required different marketing approaches. I was surprised, but my preference was clear. Of course I'd love to sell as many copies of *Disguised* as I possibly could, I'd love to have lots of readers, but what I cared about most was to talk about the men I'd come to know, what we shared, and the world of prison I'd witnessed.

I set up a conventional launch with bookstore readings and radio interviews, but I also arranged to speak at college symposia and prison arts gatherings. Wherever I could, I went into a nearby prison—there was almost always a nearby prison—to talk about the work I did at San Quentin and to share the poems of my students.

I had a full house at the Hungry Mind Bookstore in St. Paul. During the question and answer session that followed my reading, a woman introduced herself as the head of Minnesota's Department of Corrections. After the

Judith at Black Oak Books, Berkeley, on release   FAMILY ALBUM
of *Disguised as a Poem*, 2000.

reading, Sheryl Ramstad Hvass approached me and said that she wanted
me to see the work being done in the state's women's prison. Commissioner
Hvass picked me up from my sister's house, drove me to Shakopee, and
showed me herself.

In Kansas I'd been invited by Raylene Hinz-Penner to speak at a week-
end workshop at Bethel College. Raylene, a professor at the Mennonite
school, had been going into the Hutchinson Correctional Facility to teach
poetry and I visited her class there. In California, New York, Michigan,
and in so many states, there was a variety of prison art programs. Here,
in northeast Kansas, Raylene worked through no program. She'd had the
idea, talked to the warden, then just walked in and began teaching.

Buzz, Bill Cleveland—my former boss, the man who had hired me to
write the manual for artists working in California prisons— and I were the
speakers at the Bethel workshop. Our audience was a group of men and
women, from both the college and church, who were considering taking
on prison work as part of their mission. When I'd spoken about my work
before—at bookstores, in interviews, to friends—the audience listened as
individuals. At Bethel we spoke to—and were listened to by—a community.

171

The men and women considered together their shared obligation to people in prison. They asked of each other, "What's on your heart?"

The Iowa Correctional Institution for Women housed about 600 women when I visited in 2001. The entire state's prison population was under 8,000 (California's at this time was over 160,000). By the time I visited Mitchellville, I'd visited prisons in Connecticut, Kansas, Minnesota, and New York. Therefore I brought in writing, not only by my San Quentin students, but by people in prisons in these other states as well. The women looked through the various hand-made publications, reading out loud, and commenting on the poems. One said the chapbooks made her feel that she was part of a true writing community.

In Michigan, I worked with The Prison Creative Arts Project for a few days, visiting three or four prisons. I observed university students offering theater and poetry classes and taught a poetry workshop myself. At Parr Highway, a minimum-security men's institution, a large group of prisoners gathered to listen to me read from *Disguised*. I gave the reading I did in bookstores and then asked for response. The question I had been asked most often in previous Q&A sessions was, "How did your students change?" Here I was asked this question in reverse, in the form that made sense to me. Instead of being asked how my students had changed, I was asked how I had changed. This was the question Elmo's assignment had asked me to examine.

That "how did your students change?" question troubled me. Of course I understood what the questioners meant. My students had been maximum security prisoners, most of them convicted of serious crimes. Many had harmed, even killed, another human being. My questioners assumed that the purpose of sharing poetry in a place like San Quentin was to transform men from criminals into productive citizens.

Although I understood, I was also surprised. As I had written in that "Artistic Imperialism" article more than a decade before, whether working with children, elders, teenagers, or prisoners, I'd never thought my job was to change anyone. I believed, as Spoon put it, that "all rehabilitation is self-rehabilitation." So I thought for a long time about how I wanted to respond to the question. Here's what I came up with.

First I asked each person in the audience to think of the worst thing he or she had ever done. "Now imagine," I instructed, "that this act is all you're known for. Imagine that everything in your world is designed to treat you as a person defined by this act. Any other fact of your life—any act of love, creativity, compassion, intelligence, or joy—is irrelevant. You are only a person who has done this worst thing. That's it, that's you, from now till forever.

"This is the reality of a person in prison," I pointed out. "Whether you actually did that worst thing, or you didn't; whether it was one uncharacteristic act, or part of a sad series of missteps; whether you are still the person who committed that wrong, or someone whose spirit has grown—you've been convicted and you're thrown into a world where all you are is bad and ready to do bad."

I told the audience that in such an environment I was given a grant which allowed me to share poetry. I had a room in which my students could be not only prisoners, but also poets. I, and the guest artists I brought in, related to the prisoner poets as full human beings and not as men who were capable only of one worst act. I did what I could to provide a space in which other qualities—those qualities of compassion, intelligence, and joy I just mentioned—had room to live and grow.

At the same time that I was visiting prisons in other states and learning about prison arts programs nationally, my experience was also becoming more personal. Elmo and I had begun building a friendship while working on *Disguised* and in the years that followed, I visited him often. I took my place in long lines before the sun had even come up; heard stories of those who drove five hundred miles every weekend to visit a son, father, or husband; was "processed," as prison names the hoops erected for visitors to go through; sat at uncomfortable tables in crowded visiting rooms under heavy surveillance; watched little children cry when men, who seemed to be strangers but said they were daddies, scooped them on to their laps; tried to find decent and reasonably priced food in the vending machines. I listened to Elmo talk deeply about his life on the streets and in prison.

Judith with Elmo (left) and Coties, visiting room CSP-Solano, early 2000s.
VISITING ROOM PRISON PHOTOGRAPHER (POLAROID)

At Quentin I had courted that Robert Bresson wide vision in which I could see apparent contradictions as part of some larger whole. In those years, I'd consciously tried to grow a big spirit; much of *Disguised* spoke of this journey. Now, sitting so often in visiting rooms getting to know Elmo, and letting him get to know me, I found myself pulled by the particular. Point of view, always my subject, narrowed and, from this position, I was most often angry. Angry at a million things but especially—to use simplistic language for extremely complex subjects—at inequity and the misuse of power.

Misuse of power is a reality not only within prison itself. For example, just after I left San Quentin, I received a call from someone working as a researcher on what he said would be a major film. He asked if any of my former students might be willing to talk with him. I wrote a few men about his request, and Carlo Bernard began an exchange with Spoon. Spoon sent letters and poems and eventually we learned that the major film was Michael Mann's *Heat*.

A few years later, watching Mann's subsequent film, *Ali*, I heard a character speak lines from Spoon's poem, "Real."

Realness eats raw meat
and does not waver
nor drift on the currents.
He has the staying power
of the sun.
Realness walks only in his
own shoes.

The lines in *Ali* were in a different order, but there was no question that these were Spoon's words. I nearly shouted, I was so excited, and could hardly wait for the credits to roll. I waited, but Spoon's name never appeared.

At the library later that week, I looked through the new books section and there on the shelf was the script of *Ali*. Talk about cosmic! I checked the script out, photocopied the pages on which those realness lines appeared, and sent these to Spoon. Then I tracked down Carlo Bernard and Michael Mann. Spoon and I each wrote to both men, more than once, but neither has ever replied.

I'm sure filmmakers have stolen lines before, but the sin here seemed worse to me because Spoon was in prison. All Spoon owned was his experience and his writing, and though he had generously shared these, even they had been taken from him. No wonder William Henley's "Invictus" had been such a popular poem at San Quentin: "I am the master of my fate:/I am the captain of my soul!"

Inequity. I think most U.S. citizens know that black and brown men and women are incarcerated at rates profoundly out of proportion to their numbers in the population. We know this, but haven't found ways to frame many useful conversations on the subject. When I taught at the continuation high school, race was a subject the young people most often preferred to avoid talking about. Their experience had been that not much good came from such discussions. Most felt that no one could really understand what they'd gone through unless that person had undergone the same events or emotions. Sometimes—because of something that happened in school, or the response to an assignment, or a fight waiting to happen—we did have conversations, carefully structured with forms and rules. These conversations easily veered off into "my suffering is worse than yours" terrain and the adult facilitator had to find a way to balance what the teenagers called their right to free speech with maintaining a container for the talk that was as safe as it could be.

One particular that often surprised me was that many white youth felt they'd been the victims of racism. Not only did they recount how their Irish, Italian, or Jewish ancestors were treated in history, they told of hurts from their own lives. *Tony and I used to be best friends when we were little and now he ignores me on the bus because I'm not black.* These students listened to the adults' lectures on the difference between prejudice and institutional racism, but perhaps because they were living in California in 1995 instead of Mississippi in 1955, they weren't convinced. This was often the point in the conversation when they'd begin sharing the history of the potato famine or the pogroms.

I don't know why I was surprised, though, since at this same time I was volunteering with a victim-offender reconciliation program in Oakland. Through VORP, volunteers facilitated mediations between youth charged with a crime and the person the crime had been against. In the trainings we gave for volunteers, adults, too, didn't always perceive how personal prejudice, stereotypes, assumptions, and even race hatred differed from the structural racism that created first- and second-class citizens.

The summer after I finished teaching at the continuation high school, the summer before I left to write *Disguised*, one of our students was charged with murder. Steve was one of the young men in the school I'd least expected to wind up in juvenile hall. He was big and burly, and you could feel anger just below the surface, but Steve also had a capacity to think beyond his own needs and desires, unusual in a teenage boy.

Apparently Steve had spent Saturday night with his friends drinking. I wasn't there, so I don't know what happened, but his mother told us there was some mutual harassment—the boys toward a woman, the woman toward them—and the group of drunk young men attacked. Steve wasn't the one who killed the woman, but he was there when she was killed. "No man in my family has been able to handle liquor," his mother said when the school principal and I showed up to speak at Steve's arraignment.

I visited Steve in juvenile hall and the guard led me into a tiny room. I turned my back to the door's huge window of glass and sat down on one side of the room's single small table. Steve's hefty frame already filled the flimsy plastic chair on the table's other side. He had turned seventeen five days before and his tee-shirted body was certainly man-sized. But as I looked at his short-cropped hair and his pained eyes, I saw the little boy Steve had been long before I met him.

His hands shaped a V on the table between us as he described the two roads he felt forking before him. "I'm trying to stay on the right road," he said, lifting his right hand slightly. "I'm trying to live with faith. But," now it was his left hand moving, "I sometimes fall back, feel it's too hard, not worth it. I'm tempted again by this wrong road."

Steve knew he might well be on his way to Youth Authority or adult prison and this thought caused dread. He searched for words to accurately convey what he was feeling. He looked down at his two hands on the table, then up at me, "How am I going to stay on the right road here, at this place, where some inmate ticks you off and you're put in a situation where you could end up with more time?"

Although the world behind bars isn't my world, for twenty-five years now, my life has brought me in close as a witness. I've learned from those I know inside that surviving (both physically and spiritually) a long prison sentence demands many skills, including the one Steve described: Developing the capacity to observe one's responses rather than reacting with habitual emotion, a spiritual demand made of those apparently least equipped for the task. The best I could do for Steve was to ask Elmo to write him to share information and advice based on real experience.

At San Quentin an administrator had once told me, "There'll always be prisons. There'll always be parents who raise children to fill them." I know what he meant, but "parents to raise them" seems to me a shorthand for a complicated braid woven by poverty, racism, classism, absent fathers, poor education, limited job opportunities, alcohol and drug use.

Besides, neither Steve nor any man I'd known at Quentin was merely the result of some set of reasons. They were human beings. And, when I met them, they were young human beings coming up hard against their own fates.

A decade after visiting Steve at juvenile hall, I attended a death penalty trial and watched the young defendant, right there on the stand, recognize both the horror he had caused and the horror done to him when he was a child. The clichés used to describe wakening consciousness—a light bulb going off, veils lifting—speak a truth. This young man's face in the moment he saw what he had not seen before was amazing to witness.

So my heart nearly breaks as I ask: Why does it take murder and the prospect of life behind bars to wake up so many young men? Psychologists are likely to have one response to this question, sociologists another. Prison abolitionists have their reply, as do criminologists, political theorists, neuroscientists, and people in poor communities worried for their sons. While I'm sure each observer notices a piece of the truth, the input I myself am most interested in comes from the ones who used to be these young men.

Which is why I am glad for occasional visits to New Folsom, the maximum security prison where Spoon is currently housed and where Jim Carlson has been artist facilitator for over fifteen years. Pat Nolan, Spoon's friend when he was first at New Folsom in the late 1980s, was a lifer and one of those unconscious young men who woke up. Pat became relentless in his search, not for answers so much, as for ways that he and his fellow prisoners could change both themselves and the prison world that they lived in.

Now, many years after Pat's death, there is a solid group of men at New Folsom who continue his inquiry. Most participate in both a men's group Pat founded as well as in Arts-in-Corrections. These men are dedicated to increasing their own consciousness, changing their actions, and reaching out to others on the yard whom they recognize as ready for the same hard work they themselves have undertaken.

Much of what I hear these men say about their own waking up confirms and deepens my own observations. For the past number of years I've worked with WritersCorps, a program whose teaching artists share writing with young people at a variety of sites in San Francisco. The youth we work with are mostly poor, often immigrant, sometimes incarcerated. We're privileged to partner with some excellent public school teachers, smart principals, and caring program staff, but it seems to me that both youth and adults are stymied by a system that's set up against them.

At New Folsom I listen to men who once had a great deal in common with many of the children I know now. Spoon, for example, was a little boy with a rich imagination. He lay on sand dunes and looked up at the sky; he pondered what adventures the rainbows above might lead to. Spoon was curious, at home in the physical world, and open to learning. Yet adults at his school didn't see or relate to that little boy. The Spoon they noticed received paddlings instead of encouragement and negative predictions instead of invitations to discovery. Rick, another of the old timers at New Folsom, said in one of our group talks at the prison: "When I was young, if any teacher had ever invited me to put my feelings into a poem or a painting, I might not have quit school."

Of course art-making alone cannot right the world's wrongs, but we seem to be going backward or sideways. As one excellent continuation

Judith (second from right) with Janet Heller (far left)
and WritersCorps teachers, mid-2000s   KATHARINE GIN

high school teacher recently told me, "We know exactly what our students need, and none of it is measured by test scores."

Our civic conversations about how to increase the odds that all children will succeed are often contentious, partisan, and emotional. But I don't see even those who sincerely believe in the value of standards sending their own children to a school whose learning environment is entirely shaped by high stakes testing. Parents who have a choice choose schools that understand intelligence as multi-faceted, schools that create a wide variety of approaches to the process of learning and critical thinking. Parents who have a choice don't choose schools such as the one WritersCorps worked at for ten years whose principal suddenly decreed that only the top five percent of students (as measured by test scores) would be allowed any art during the school day. My observation—after a lifetime working in public schools and prisons—is that, whether by design or unintended consequence, some of our children are being educated to assume power, while others are being trained for prison.

The phrase "prison industrial complex" is often associated with Angela Davis, but Ms. Davis isn't the only one describing politicians who fan fear about crime in an attempt to win votes, voters swayed by these fears, prison guards intent on job security, and business people seeing a buck to be made off people in prison and their families. Nor is Ms. Davis the only one noting the ways in which the link between these forces has resulted in our country having the highest documented incarceration rate in the world. Joseph T. Hallinan makes similar points, for example, in his *Going Up the River: Travels in a Prison Nation*. Mr. Hallinan is formerly with *The Wall Street Journal*—hardly a radical rag. I hoped voters would respond sensibly to information about the consequences of the choices our nation is making. I thought when citizens realized the percentage of our state budgets being spent on prison—and therefore not on education, health care, and other social services—we'd demand change. Federally, and in some states, this is beginning to happen. In California, however, what little positive change is arriving has been a result of federal court mandate rather than voter or legislative initiative.

For almost twenty-five years I've watched Spoon develop from near-silence into a prolific writer, performer, and teacher. His poems have been the subject of movies, set to music, and studied by college students. I feel awe at all Spoon has accomplished. I consider it wasteful—to his spirit and to California's state budget—that Spoon remains behind bars. And also I wonder who Spoon might be if his talents had been nurtured when he was a small, curious boy. Might the person he murdered still be alive? What unknown Spoon-given beauty might exist in the world?

I think often of Spoon's "one foot in light and one foot in darkness," about Steve's two hands on the table, and about what Lynnelle said when I interviewed her for the manual Bill Cleveland hired me to write. Speaking of the men on death row, Lynnelle told me, "The men that I work with have done horrible things. But in their work with me they are funny, bright, creative, and caring human beings who often make beautiful art. I can't reconcile these facts. All I can do is hold them in my two hands."

Me, too. I pray to hold in my hands the paradoxical whole.

Richard Shelton began sharing poetry in Arizona prisons in the early 1970s. His beautiful memoir, *Crossing the Yard: Thirty Years as a Prison Volunteer*, closes at the end of a workshop in which nearly all his students report that they're going to be transferred, many of them to private prisons in other states where there will be no support for the good work they have been doing. They're being transferred, as Spoon was from San Quentin, for no sensible reason at all, and there's nothing Shelton can do to stop it. The last line of *Crossing the Yard* says better than I've ever heard said what my prison arts friends and colleagues feel when we speak to each other of what we've experienced and witnessed: "I want to put my head down on the table in front of me and weep with a pain that will not be comforted and a rage I cannot express."

16

The Circle

THE MAD, BLACK CAPTAIN back on B-Yard, Pleasant Valley State Prison, had tried to transfer me to Salinas Valley, a level four prison where there was violence and wasn't programming. Instead I was sent back to New Folsom—California State Prison-Sacramento.

At New Folsom I sat in an empty cell by myself, which was cool. Jim Carlson, now artist facilitator here, brought some books and paper by. I had not seen Jim in over sixteen years, since *Waiting for Godot* days. We had one of our longest conversations ever. We were both grayer, thinner, and perhaps even wiser. I did not know what to expect going back to a level four prison, but I sat primed for anything—wars, long lockdowns, and isolation. I also knew that in the midst of whatever madness existed at New Folsom, with brother Jim Carlson there, there would be a vibrant Arts-in-Corrections program.

After the success of our short film, *Three Poems by Spoon Jackson*, Michel and Albin were given funds by the Swedish Film Institute to come back to America to do a longer documentary film on me and my life. I was still on A-Yard at Pleasant Valley at this time, and the white captain seemed open to the film project and told Michel and me to submit a proposal. We did. The prison turned us down, saying they could not have a film that focused on one prisoner. The same old spin about something positive being negative, the same old bullshit about setting prisoners up as heroes. I did not give up, though. I had Michel contact Jim through Judith. I knew if anyone could part seas or move mountains it was Jim, the man who helped bring *Waiting for Godot* to San Quentin.

Pleasant Valley had been festering with Valley Fever, a mutated fungus from years of pesticide use. The fever attacked and destroyed the body as AIDS did, killing the immune system. We understood that Valley Fever traveled on dust particles in the air, so it was doubly hazardous to one's health to come outdoors when the wind blew. Also, there were nests of brown spiders lurking in boxes, corners, and most dark places. I don't know if they were true brown recluse spiders or not, but whatever kind of spiders they were, the result of their bites was a person's flesh being eaten up. So perhaps it was a blessing to be away from Pleasant Valley State Prison.

I was shocked by how open New Folsom had become. I couldn't remember any of the things that went on when I arrived in 2004 being true when I resided at the prison in the late 1980s. We were now fed in the cells and no longer walked to the chow halls. Back in the day, when something jumped in the chow hall, bullets bounced off walls and metal tables like racket balls hitting everything and anyone. Bullets often went through one person and hit another.

Everything seemed smaller than it was when I was here the first time. The yard, cell blocks, and cages had seemed much bigger in those days. There were no boundary lines on the yard then, you could drink from any water fountain and sit almost anywhere on the yard. Now the yard was sectioned off by race and gang. Yet, New Folsom was way more peaceful than it had been the first time. When I was here before, the blacks and Southern Mexicans could hardly tolerate each other without fighting. Now some of them moved and spoke as if they were old friends.

My old poet friend, Pat Nolan, had died from Hepatitis C, but I met a new artist, Marty Williams, who had been Pat's cellie. The two were like brothers. Marty filled me in on Pat's death, how Hep C had grown inside Pat's body like tapeworms eating his vital organs before any cure could stop them. Marty told me how Pat had helped found a men's group at New Folsom that promoted peace and harmony between the races, encouraging the men to dialog and share their own inner spirits and injured souls. Marty spoke of how Pat wanted to start an Arts-in-Corrections newsletter but never got the chance. Marty refused to let Pat's memory die and, in that spirit, he founded the AIC newsletter, *The Ugly Shoe*, which featured poems and essays by Pat.

Yes, I missed my old friend, Pat. When I left him back in the early 1990s, I thought we would meet again, inside or outside prison. Brother Pat faced an end physically and progressively painful, like being eaten alive by wolves. Yet I knew that his spirit, his poet's freedom and ken, would allow him to soar even years after his death, and that thanks to Marty, Pat's poems and words would never die.

The connection between me and Pat continued when Jim asked me to teach the poetry class Pat had once taught. Before I allowed Jim to turn the class over to me, though, I went into my silent mode to observe people, the prison, the yard, and the AIC programs. I sat in silence in the poetry class for a few months in the same room where Diana Henning had long ago taught Pat and me about annotations.

The first Arts-in-Corrections guest I read for was a songwriter, poet, and performer from Alaska named Buddy Tabor. I then read for a young soulful rock group, Flow Motion. Also from Alaska, a brilliant goddess, spoken word poet, slam award-winning artist and radio personality named Corina Delgado bounced into the Arts-in-Corrections room. I often played Corina's CD as an example of how poetry flows. Her soul-hugging verse quickly and naturally became part of my curriculum. Cheri Snook, an announcer and producer at radio station KVMR 89.5 FM, and her daughter, Korina, constructed this bridge from the station's home in Nevada City to New Folsom's Arts-in-Corrections. Working with Jim Carlson, she brought many great artists, poets, and singers inside. All of the artists came because of my sister Cheri's dedication to lay brick across the darkness between the prison and the free world and to create a circle.

Over my years at New Folsom singer, songwriter, activist, and poet, Diane Patterson, has become a frequent visitor to the writing classes I teach. I had the tremendous honor of opening up a Thanksgiving concert for Diane and her sister goddesses, Melissa Mitchell and Kimberly Bass. The main feature that day was international recording artist brother Michael Franti and Spearhead. They left the opening of Mohammad Ali's library to give the concert in New Folsom's chapel. All these realness people reminded me of the artists I encountered back at San Quentin: Bill Irwin, Czelsaw Milosz, Barney Rosset, Ruth Gendler, Martin Esslin, and Kate Dougherty. Kate, Barney, and Bill are still in touch with me.

I had not envisioned being transferred back up to a level four prison. I had not seen it coming as I basked in the sunshine of level three prisons. I had not foreseen being so heavily involved in Arts-in-Corrections again, or working with Jim Carlson so long after we did *Waiting for Godot* at San Quentin. Though Jim had sent word to me once, when I was still housed at CMC-East, letting me know that he wanted me to come to New Folsom and run the poetry class. I had told Jim that was not going to happen unless he moved to work at a lower level prison. Yet here I was at New Folsom, not only participating in Arts-in-Corrections, but running two writing groups as a teaching artist.

Often I create my lessons in the moment, sometimes just before the class starts. The lesson might be something I learned from Judith, Dianna Henning, or a combination of both. Sometimes a lesson comes from an exercise I have gleaned from a book or from my days studying acting; other times a lesson develops on the spot from a student's question. I usually start the class with a ten minute silent free writing session, though these sometimes last thirty minutes or longer, depending on the pencil movements on paper. Most of the time, my students recognize the significance of the silence, of having this rare and sacred writing space to unfold their inner worlds of poetry and prose, those things that have lain dormant or hidden in their hearts and souls. Their pens burst forth in the silence like seeds before the sunlight hits them.

One lesson I created is called "Questions." For example: What does war taste like? What is the color of love? What does peace sound like? What does child abuse look like? What does revenge feel like? What does forgiveness smell like? I make all the questions in the moment just before class starts. I try to ask them in unusual ways. I write each question on a big sheet of paper and let each student pick one randomly.

Sometimes I start a class with a heated discussion on subjects like absent fatherhood, spousal abuse, racism, child abuse, crime and punishment, and even religion and politics. I strive to have all colors of people in my group and to get them to express their different cultures. When the talk flows its course, I have the class write about and explore that passion they put into their speeches. Some guys need topics to get them going, so I provide them with wise sayings or read poetry from books.

I've gone to Adult Basic Education classes to do writing workshops. It's easy to know when someone in the group cannot read or write because he will often be very outgoing and will encourage others to read or write without writing a poem himself. I learned somewhere how to do group poems. I give out a subject—say love—and we go around the group and have each student say a line. Either I write the line down or some of the students do the writing. Then someone reads the poem that we created aloud. This gives the student who can't read or write a chance to be part of the workshop.

At New Folsom, I sit on a top bunk, surrounded by papers and books, the hub of my little world. There I write and plan lessons. I wonder how round my life circle will be and hope it will circle me back to the streets and to physical freedom.

Meanwhile the circle continues to go both backward and forward. I heard from Saga after over ten years. She filled in the blanks, letting me know what she had been doing. She had her own little art company and website. Before Saga went back to Sweden, I had dedicated my poem, "Powder Love," to her and to our relationship. Barney Rosset, famed publisher and old friend of Samuel Beckett, liked my work. Barney published a few poems I'd written that had been inspired by, or that were in tribute to, Beckett after he passed away in the late '80s. Barney still suggests places to send my work, and he included the love poem I'd written for Saga in his evergreen.com web magazine. Saga saw the poem and decided she wanted the dedication line off, so she contacted Barney's web magazine editor who declined to remove the line.

In "Powder Love," I had spoken of signing our names on a sandy beach. When Saga went back to Sweden, she did that and sent me a photo. So when she asked me to contact Barney and have the dedication line removed, it shocked me like being slapped repeatedly in the chest by a baseball bat. Saga did not want to be connected to me. She had a son who was sixteen, and Saga wrote that she did not want him to go online and see a love poem dedicated to his mother. Saga's letter made me wonder what had happened to the rebel Swedish woman I had married; I wondered how the rebel had become conservative.

I did not tell Saga how deeply her request hurt me until after I contacted Barney Rosset and had his people take out the line. I then wrote and told Saga the poem was a tribute to our love and that it saddened me to take that line out. I have not heard from Saga again, though I still have the sweet memories of how our eyes met and our secret love blossomed in silence, in

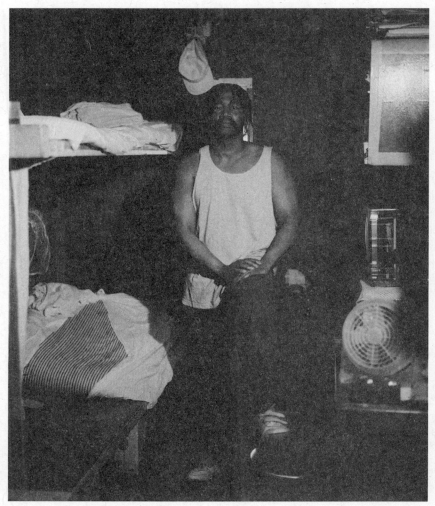

Spoon in cell, New Folsom, 2005.   ALBIN BIBLOM

a room in a prison full of people, where it was hard to restrain myself from taking her hand and going to some obviously blind spot on the dungeon floor of the education building to make love. I often had to put that passion Saga inspired in me into a poem.

Poem lines continue to help sustain me, particularly in times of internal pain of the heart and soul. The flow of some lines from "Song of Myself" is like elephants marching in a single file. Whitman's lines set my spirit free and give it wings to glide beyond prison walls, give me strength to bear prison conditions. The lines help me travel back to the days I ran the dry river with semi-wild dogs.

At CMC, I sat at the base of a concrete light pole and watched bees larger than the wildflowers they sought to sip from in the patches of brownish grass. To my left, I heard small grunting sounds and I saw a late blooming red-breasted finch trying to fly away. But he seemed caught in a bind, not knowing how to fly or run away. So he just rolled and tumbled on the ground, flapping his wings and legs. I turned and fed the sparrows as they floated down so lovely from the feeding tree. A misty, warm rain shimmered down from dark clouds. When the sky is dark and there is light rain, the sparrows are more trusting and amorous toward humans. Hundreds of sparrows gathered at my feet huddling together like baby rabbits. Some birds fluttered up, taking bread from my fingertips. A newcomer was there, a female—a pastel white or tannish brown. She reminded me of Saga. She glowed among all the other sparrows, even the male sparrows that Mother Earth had blessed with all the colors. She kept her distance.

At dusk, I watched the turkey vultures circle high in the sky for more than two hours. One by one, they circled a large stand of evergreen trees just outside the prison. As night hit harder, each vulture landed in the trees, but only one bird circled above the evergreens at a given time. The darker it became, the less each bird revolved. I wondered why they circled the trees before landing. I felt my heart take a deep breath as the last bird descended. I thought of Whitman's lines:

...I think I could turn and live with animals
they are so placid and self-contained,
I stand and look at them long and long
They do not sweat and whine about their condition

More no detour straight to the heart lines for me are these from "Dover Beach" by Matthew Arnold:

Ah, love, let us be true
To one another! For the world, which seems
To lie before us like a land of dreams,
So various, so beautiful, so new
Hath really neither joy, nor love, nor light
Nor certitude, nor peace, nor help for pain:...

Spoon outside the Arts-in-Corrections room, New Folsom, 2005.   ALBIN BIBLOM

A guy in my poetry class once tried to steal that stanza, not knowing that those lines had traveled in my heart through three prisons. After he read, I gave him a chance to back down from his assertion that he created those lines. But he persisted, even after I told him that "Dover Beach" was in an anthology right there in the AIC library. I showed him the stanza in Arnold's poem, yet the guy still did not seem to get it.

The poem and those lines often soothed my sad heart after a break up or after hearing someone try to justify war. I still well up sometimes when I read them. The lines let me know that there is no good side or good guys in war, that all war is insidious like flesh-eating fungus. There are so many gates one could step through into these lines and find solace. The lines seep into the soul like rainwater in a meadow and nourish different plants and flowers to blossom at different times.

My Swedish brother, Jan Jonson, continues to travel through Sweden and Europe telling the story of Samuel Beckett, *Godot*, and of me on stage. Jan's performances last four to six hours. Jan recently came to Arts-in-

Corrections here at New Folsom along with a talented French Canadian film maker, Michka, who had done a film on the Kumla prisoners' *Waiting for Godot*, a film titled *Prisoners of Beckett*. I had not seen Jan in close to twenty years. Michka wants to do a documentary film on where the actors are now after doing *Waiting for Godot* at San Quentin. Jan brought scripts of Samuel Beckett's *Endgame*, and gave a two-day acting workshop using that text. Jan said that Beckett told him Hamm and Clov in *Endgame* were continuations of Pozzo and Lucky from *Godot*.

I felt good and natural to be acting again with Jan; it was like old times, when I started performing at San Quentin. I felt the power and the magic of Beckett and the theater unfolding in my heart and soul. I also stood back at times and watched Jan direct. Jan wanted me to do more acting, but I wanted to learn from Jan's unmatched brilliance as a director.

Jan hoped to do *Endgame*, with himself and me as the main characters. This was a promise Jan had made to Beckett before his death. Unlike the first time I acted, now I was totally open to playing Pozzo as Hamm. The circles continue to move backwards and forward, yet there seems to be no possibility of performing *Endgame* at New Folsom or most other prisons due to no space or support by the California Department of Corrections and Rehabilitation. Arts-in-Corrections's funding has been cut, and come January 2010, the program is scheduled to be abolished.

Another Swedish brother, Stefan Säfsten, a conductor and composer, has brought life to my poetry through music. Stefan and his wife, Lena, and the Järva Röster choir gave a small concert tour in the United States to promote *Freedom for the Prisoners*, the CD Stefan created of my poems set to his music. Stefan and I created our second project, *Words of Realness* and the release of that CD was also followed by performances of the work.

How do I hold a sunny day in my heart? How do I speak about the performance of *Words of Realness* that just took place here inside New Folsom Prison on the small yard not more than a week ago? What words can embrace the voice, the music, and sound that angels would hold dear? To have sat on the grass and watched the prisoners and some prison staff enjoy an unprecedented concert event, simply as people enjoying a show, freed my spirit and heart and reminded me of our last night at San Quentin performing *Waiting for Godot* when I sat in the audience to share the last scenes. Järva Röster, Sounds Found Orchestra, and conductor, Stefan, brought inside New Folsom and left inside New Folsom beauty behind cell bars. I felt finally at home, at home with my Swedish people as we spoke, smiled, and laughed.

My poems connect with other prisoners, some from as far away as Estonia and Russia. I have gotten letters from both places. And students in American criminal justice classes and college prison literature classes have written me to help them with their term papers after they've read Judith's book, *Disguised as a Poem*.

I long to travel and poet with Judith as she crosses the USA appearing in colleges, schools, workshops, and as she works with other helpful programs. I long to travel to Sweden, Norway, and elsewhere with Jan reading my poetry as he does his performance. I long to travel across Europe and the globe with brother Stefan doing our music project.

Judith and Jan taught and shared their crafts from their own truth, from their hearts and souls. This is probably the only thing Judith, my writing mentor, and Jan, my acting mentor, have in common. Both are masters at what they do, and by their doings, others are able to learn and be inspired from the inside out to do their own thing. Judith and Jan work with voice, one silent and the other spoken. Both inspired me to embrace, and get out of the way of, my own flow.

If I had to learn or be taught to be a poet, I would have surely failed, as I had in all my pre-prison schooling. I had to unlearn and unknow to be a poet and to get out of the way of the muses or inspiration and let the poet be a poet inside me. In silence, a poet is still a poet—no words. I think as kids we touch the poet flow before we are jaded by society, environment, prejudices, and biases. So even without words, a poet would still be a poet with grunts, gestures, and silences, as surely as a cloud is still a cloud when there is no rain.

So I don't believe anyone can be taught to be a poet, either you are or you are not. Technical information and figurative language can be pointed out, but talent and inspiration is an unknown and natural thing in poets, as natural as for birds to sing and lions to roar. If Judith had been a dictator type poet or teacher, that approach would not have worked for me. I would have rebelled and bucked the authority. Yet sometimes I am an angry, impatient teaching artist. When I realize it later, or see it in one of my student's eyes, I get pissed at myself. It feels like I have no one to share these feelings with. Judith wrote me something wise after I spoke out passionately in an Arts-in-Corrections group she recently visited: "If you're just expressing your anger and frustration, that's cool (real). But there's no response to someone's emotion other than to make room for it."

Sometimes I am so angry inside that I don't hear myself, I don't see myself, and don't hear or see anybody else. I must remember the words of Fo-sho-hing-tsan-king, "Conquer your foe by force, you increase his enmity. Conquer by love, and you will reap no after sorrow," and the Haitian proverb: "Rocks in the water don't know the misery of rocks in the sun."

Sometimes, now that I am a known poet, writer, and also a teaching artist, I am called on to speak, to be heard. Judith, Jim, and others often tell me that the world wants to hear what I have to say and my spirit sometimes knows that to be true. Still, sometimes my shadow side gets in the way and doesn't allow me to hear my spirit's call to words. My indignation at still being incarcerated after so long sometimes gets in my way because I believe my work, my voice, and my presence could be more effective and inspiring from the free world. I could touch hands, look into eyes, tell stories, and encourage people in a more direct way to walk in their own shoes. I could touch more hearts and spirits in deeper ways outside of prison.

Sometimes I get pissed at a prison system that strives to set people up to fail, even when some prisoners work night and day to be real and successful, even when some prisoners push to help heal and not hinder or destroy. One example is the project a college professor and I set up with all his white, upper middle-class students in upstate New York who had no true concept of prisons or prisoners. We had his Persuasive Writing class students write men in the class I teach a series of questions on restorative justice versus retributive justice. After the letter exchange, the college students were shocked that prisoners were human, just as they were, shocked that we had thoughts, feelings, dreams, and some form of mental and physical abuse in common. Some college students related to me in my silence.

I do not use silence as a refuge, or out of fear, or to run. Silence has always been as precious to me as walking, breathing, or dreaming, and has saved my life and heart more than once. Silence has enabled me to go through great loss and pain with my head up and without pride. I choose silence sometimes out of respect, so that I can listen and grow, and so that I won't disrupt the flow of a group or workshop, especially when the session seems to be progressing the way people want it to go. Other times I just don't have anything to say; nothing I could offer would improve on the poetry of silence.

Sometimes in prison, where I have no space, I am in a group and feel like I need to leave the room before I say something stupid, call someone out on something I think or know to be bullshit, or just want to get away from people. Although my feelings are strong, I have no right to do that. What I consider bullshit may be flowers and gardens to someone else. I know that whoever said what I judged not true still has every right to say his piece. Also when everyone is agreeing on everything, blowing kisses and hugs each other's way, I sometimes feel or think that I must bring another route or truth out and perhaps shed some doubt.

I see these badger-like traits in myself and continue to work on my mind, body, and soul. I strive to maintain my spirit and heart, to keep love flowing and creativity true. Yes there is some anger, bitterness, and hope-lessness as I live inside a monster prison system that has been condemned almost everywhere in the world except within its own boundaries. But I find and build freedom by living in the moment. This allows the warmth and light in my soul and heart to flow through my poetry and prose and gives me something to share.

Forging my path in life is a melancholic mixture of wonder and sadness. I am not happy, nor will I ever be happy, in prison. All I can say is what my character Pozzo said in lines Judith, Jim, Denise, and Jan often quoted during our development of the play: "That's how it is on this bitch of an earth." I will be released from prison one day, by a beautiful real life or by a beautiful real death. In either case, I have found my niche in life which is something not even death can take away.

Resources

Both Judith and Spoon have websites.

judithtannenbaum.com
spoonjackson.com

Judith's site has links to a great deal of information on teaching arts and prison arts.

Readers can write Spoon (please enclose postage for return letter):

Spoon Jackson B-92377
CSP-Sac C8-125
Box 290066
Represa, CA 95671-0066

Judith's *Disguised as a Poem* tells of the years she shared with Spoon—and all her students—at San Quentin. You can read poems by the men in her class on the prison arts page of her website.

Community Arts

Community arts is a term used for decades to describe work done by artists who share art-making with people in community settings. The best source for information about the history and practice of community arts is Community Arts Network (communityarts.net).

Useful texts include: *Art and Upheaval: Artists on the World's Frontlines*, William Cleveland, New Village Press, 2008; *Art in Other Places: Artists at Work in America's Community and Social Institutions*, William Cleveland, Praeger Publishers, 2000; *Beginner's Guide to Community-Based Arts*, Keith

Knight and Mat Schwarzman, New Village Press, 2005; *New Creative Community: The Art of Cultural Development*, Arlene Goldbard, New Village Press, 2006; *Reimaging America: The Arts of Social Change*, edited by Mark O'Brien and Craig Little, New Society Press, 1990; *The Citizen Artist: 20 Years of Art in the Public Arena*, edited by Linda Frye Burnham and Steven Durland, Critique Press, 1998.

Teaching Arts

Teaching arts is a relatively new phrase sometimes used interchangeably with community arts and sometimes used to describe the work of artists sharing with young people, primarily in school settings. A comprehensive source of information is the Association of Teaching Artists (teachingartists .com). *Teaching Artist Journal* is the peer-reviewed journal for the field.

WritersCorps, the program Judith currently works with, is one example of an excellent program (writerscorps.org). For a full description of another great program, see *AIMprint: New Relationships in the Arts and Learning*, Cynthia Weiss and Amanda Leigh Lichtenstein, Columbia College Chicago, 2008.

Prison and Prison Arts

The single best resource for anyone wanting to teach art in prison is *Creativity Held Captive: Guidelines for Working With Artists in Prison*, Patricia McConnel, Logoria Books, 2005 (creativityheldcaptive.com). Other helpful guides are PEN American Center's *Handbook for Writers in Prison* and *Words Over Walls: Starting a Writing Workshop in a Prison*, Hettie Jones and Janine Pommy Vega; and *Teaching the Arts behind Bars*, Rachel Marie-Crane Williams, Northeastern University Press, 2003. Judith's *Manual for Artists Working in Prison* can be downloaded from her website.

PEN American Center's Prison Writing Program offers an annual contest for prisoner writers (pen.org). The Prison Arts Coalition blog site allows conversation and shared information among people sharing art in and around correctional settings (theprisonartscoalition.wordpress.com).

An extensive list of prison arts programs nationally (prisonarts.info) or—in book form—*Creating Behind the Razor Wire: Perspectives from Arts in Corrections in the United States*, Krista Brune (lulu.com) 2008.

The Prison Creative Arts Project, referred to in *By Heart*, is a great prison arts program. PCAP's founder, Buzz Alexander, has written a most important history: *William Martinez Not Our Brother?: Twenty Years of the Prison Creative Arts Project,* University of Michigan Press, 2010.

Programs are often asked to provide statistics on whether prisoners participating in arts classes have a decreased incidence of disciplinary actions and/or lower rates of recidivism. The Brewster Report, one of the earliest studies, is available on Judith's website.

Anthologies that feature prisoner art and writing include: *Cellblock Visions: Prison Art in America,* edited by Phyllis Kornfield, Princeton University Press, 1997; *Couldn't Keep It to Myself: Testimonies from Our Imprisoned Sisters,* Wally Lamb and the Women of York Correctional Institution, HarperCollins, 2003; *Doing Time: 25 Years of Prison Writing,* edited by Bell Gale Chevigny, Arcade Publishing, 1999; *I'll Fly Away: Further Testimonies from the Women of York Prison,* edited by Wally Lamb, Harper, 2007; *Light From Another Country: Poetry from American Prisons,* edited by Joseph Bruchac, Greenfield Review Press, 1984; *Prison Writing in 20th-Century America,* edited by H. Bruce Franklin, Penguin, 1998; *This Prison Where I Live: The PEN Anthology of Imprisoned Writers,* edited by Siobhan Dowd, Cassell Academic, 1996; *Undoing Time: American Prisoners in Their Own Words,* edited by Jeff Evans, Northeastern University Press, 2000; *Wall Tappings: Women's Prison Writings, 200 AD to the Present,* edited by Judith Scheffler, The Feminist Press at CUNY, 2nd edition, 2002.

Anthologies that feature writing by both people in prison and their teachers: *The Funhouse Mirror: Reflections on Prison,* Robert Ellis Gordon, Washington State University Press, 2000; *Only The Dead Can Kill: Stories from Jail,* edited by Margo Perin, Community Works/West, 2006; *The Soul Knows No Bars: Inmates Reflect on Life, Death, & Hope,* Drew Leder, Rowman & Littlefield Publishers, 2000.

Recent books by people in (or formerly in) prison: *A Place to Stand,* Jimmy Santiago Baca, Grove Press, 2002; *A Question of Freedom: A Memoir of Learning, Survival, and Coming of Age in Prison,* R. Dwayne Betts, Avery, 2009; *Finding Freedom: Writings from Death Row,* Jarvis Jay Masters, Padma Publishing, 1997; *How You Lose: A Novel in Stories* by J.C. Amberchele, Carroll & Graf, 2002; *Mother California: A Story of Redemption Behind Bars,* Kenneth E. Hartman, Atlas & Co., 2009; *Sing Soft, Sing Loud,* Patricia McConnel, Logoria Books, 1995; *That Bird Has My Wings: The Autobiography of an Innocent Man on Death Row,* Jarvis Jay Masters, HarperOne, 2009; *Time of Grace: Thoughts on Nature, Family, and the Politics of Crime and Punishment,* Ken Lamberton,

University of Arizona Press, 2007; *Wilderness and Razor Wire: A Naturalist's Observations from Prison,* Ken Lamberton, Mercury House, 1999.

A few of the many well-known writers who have served time and written about it: Jack Henry Abbott, Nelson Algren, Daniel Berrigan, Philip Berrigan, Malcolm Braly, Edward Bunker, Rubin "Hurricane" Carter, Eldridge Cleaver, Angela Davis, Fyodor Dostoesvsky, Jean Genet, Emma Goldman, Vaclav Havel, Chester Himes, George Jackson, Mumia Abu-Jamal, Martin Luther King Jr., Etheridge Knight, Nazim Hikmet, O'Henry, Miguel Piñero, Irina Ratuskinskaya, Bobby Seale, Iceberg Slim, Agnes Smedley, Piri Thomas, Henry David Thoreau, Jacobo Timerman, Voltaire, Malcolm X.

In addition to Judith's *Disguised as a Poem,* recent books written by (or about) those who have taught in prison, jail, or youth institutions include: *Crossing the Yard: Thirty Years as a Prison Volunteer,* Richard Shelton, University of Arizona Press, 2007; *Imagining Medea: Rhodessa Jones and Theater for Incarcerated Women,* Rena Faden, The University of North Carolina Press, 2000; *Shakespeare Behind Bars: The Power of Drama In a Women's Prison,* Jean Trounstine, St. Martins Press, 2001; *True Notebooks: A Writer's Year at Juvenile Hall,* Mark Salzman, Vintage, 2004.

A few books on various aspects of prison: *All Alone in the World: Children of the Incarcerated,* Nell Bernstein, New Press, 2005; *Going Up the River: Travels in a Prison Nation,* Joseph T. Hallinan, Random House, 2001; *Incarceration Nation: Investigative Prison Poems of Hope and Terror,* Stephen J. Hartnett, Alta Mira Press, 2003; *The Oxford History of the Prison: The Practice of Punishment in Western Society,* edited by Norval Morris and David J. Rothman, Oxford University Press USA, 1997; *The Rise and Fall of California's Radical Prison Movement,* Eric Cummins, Stanford University Press, 1994; and *With Liberty for Some: 500 Years of Imprisonment in America*, Scott Christianson, Northeastern University Press, 1998.

About the Authors

Judith Tannenbaum has taught poetry in a wide variety of settings from primary school classrooms to maximum security prisons. She has written widely about this work in journals including *PMLA* and *Teaching Artist Journal.* Among her books are the memoir, *Disguised as a Poem: My Years Teaching Poetry at San Quentin;* two books for teachers— *Teeth, Wiggly as Earthquakes: Writing Poetry in the Primary Grades* and (with Valerie Chow Bush) *Jump Write In! Creative Writing Exercises for Diverse Communities, Grades 6-12;* and six poetry collections.

In California, Judith created Arts-in-Corrections' newsletter, wrote their book-length *Manual for Artists Working in Prison,* and developed the *Handbook for Arts in the Youth Authority Program.* She has also completed a feasibility study for arts programming in Minnesota state prisons; chaired panels and served as keynote speaker at many conferences on prison, prison arts, and teaching arts; and taught in prisons in eight states.

Judith currently serves as training coordinator for WritersCorps in San Francisco.

Spoon Jackson has been in the art world and in prison for over twenty years. He is an internationally known poet, writer, and actor, and is also a teaching artist and native flute player. His poems are collected in *Longer Ago* and have been featured in films, plays, articles, books, and music suites (most recently, *Words of Realness*, on a cd released in Sweden).

He teaches two creative writing classes at New Folsom prison in California. He has mentored entire classrooms in Sweden and Norway, writing each student individual letters. His work has become a beacon, inspiring people to walk in their own shoes.

Spoon has won four awards from the PEN Prison Writing Program: in poetry, nonfiction, fiction, and memoir. He was featured in Swedish film-maker, Michel Wenzer's, short film *Three Poems by Spoon Jackson*, which won awards in five countries.

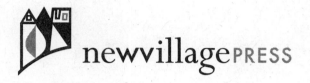
newvillagePRESS

The book you are holding was brought to you by New Village Press, the first publisher to serve the emerging field of community building. Communities are the cauldron of social change, and the healthiest changes rise from the grassroots. New Village publications focus on creative, citizen initiated works— good news and inspiring tools for growth.

If you enjoyed *By Heart* you may be interested in other books we offer about arts and social justice:

Art and Upheaval: Artists on the World's Frontlines, by William Cleveland

New Creative Community, by Arlene Goldbard

Building Commons and Community, by Karl Linn

Arts for Change: Teaching Outside the Frame, by Beverly Naidus

Undoing the Silence: Six Tools for Social Change Writing, by Louise Dunlap

Works of Heart: Building Village through the Arts,
    edited by Lynne Elizabeth and Suzanne Young

Doing Time in the Garden: Life Lessons Through Prison Horticulture,
    by James Jiler

*Performing Communities: Grassroots Ensemble Theaters Deeply Rooted
in Eight U.S. Communities,* by Robert Leonard & Ann Kilkelly;
    Linda Frye Burnham, editor

Beginner's Guide to Community-Based Arts, by Mat Schwarzman,
    Keith Knight, Ellen Forney and others

New Village Press is the publishing arm of Architects/Designers/Planners for Social Responsibility, **www.adpsr.org**, an educational nonprofit working for peace, environmental protection, social justice and the development of healthy communities.

See what else we publish: **www.newvillagepress.net**